VEGAN CHINESE COOKBOOK

VEGAN CHINESE COOKBOOK

75 DELICIOUS PLANT-BASED FAVORITES

BY YANG YANG

Photography by Elysa Weitala

ROCKRIDGE
PRESS

To my amazing mother, Yanli Yang—
your unconditional love propels me forward.

For general information on our other products and services or to obtain technical support, please contact our Customer Care Department within the United States at (866) 744-2665, or outside the United States at (510) 253-0500.

Rockridge Press publishes its books in a variety of electronic and print formats. Some content that appears in print may not be available in electronic books, and vice versa.

TRADEMARKS: Rockridge Press and the Rockridge Press logo are trademarks or registered trademarks of Callisto Media Inc. and/or its affiliates, in the United States and other countries, and may not be used without written permission. All other trademarks are the property of their respective owners. Rockridge Press is not associated with any product or vendor mentioned in this book.

Interior and Cover Designer: Karmen Lizzul
Art Producer: Samantha Ulban
Editor: Georgia Freedman
Production Editor: Ellina Litmanovich
Production Manager: Riley Hoffman

Photography © 2021 Elysa Weitala. Food Styling by Victoria Woollard. Illustrations © 2021 Tom Bingham.

Paperback ISBN: 978-1-63807-306-2
eBook ISBN: 978-1-63807-185-3
R0

CONTENTS

INTRODUCTION

At the age of 19, I moved to Canada from China, where I had spent nearly two decades of my life in the heart of the capital city, Beijing. There I grew up at the foot of the Forbidden City, went to one of the country's most prestigious schools, and watched my hometown transform into a modern metropolis. Beijing is a bustling cultural center where various Chinese subcultures, traditions, and modern influence meet. Thanks to my mother, who was an adventurous foodie, I sampled regional cuisines from across China.

My love for cooking started in my childhood, too. My grandparents had a tradition of making and eating dumplings every Sunday afternoon. I remember proudly rolling out dumpling wrappers so my family of three generations could wrap dumplings together. I enjoyed helping around the kitchen and learning a trick or two from every adult I deemed a good cook. I have fond memories of experimenting with new dishes with my uncle Hongbo. Later in life, my cooking became an important creative outlet and a type of meditation therapy during a time of illness, when I had to be very careful with what I ate. During this time, I recognized that food that suits others may not be right for you and that we must listen to our bodies to learn which foods are the best for our health. For this reason, although I am not vegan myself, I am glad to support others who want to cook vegan dishes, whether as a lifestyle choice, as part of a period of healing, or simply to diversify an omnivorous diet.

In compiling these vegan recipes, I wanted to represent the major subcuisines from across many different regions of China and to showcase a variety of Chinese cooking techniques. Most of these dishes are well-known classics, and a subset represent Chinese Buddhist vegan cooking traditions.

The process of writing this vegan Chinese cookbook has been an exciting and humbling experience for me. It was an honor to work on this project and to share the foods and culture I grew up with. At the same time, while working on this book, I realized how limited my knowledge initially was of the vast culture, deep history, and complex art of Chinese cooking. I am in awe of the rich trove of vegan recipes offered in Chinese cuisine.

The Vegan Chinese Kitchen

While cooking the dishes in this book, you may see ingredients, cooking techniques, and equipment that are entirely new to you. This section of the book offers an overview of vegan Chinese cooking to help you familiarize yourself with common Chinese ingredients, tools, and techniques. Using the guide below, you will be able to properly stock your vegan Chinese kitchen so that you can make authentic dishes right at home.

Veganism and Chinese Cooking

A few hundred to a thousand years ago in China, meats were only available for special occasions or for very wealthy people. So, not surprisingly, many classic traditional Chinese dishes are entirely plant-based. And, as it happens, Chinese cooking has also never really used dairy products. The rich flavors of vegan Chinese dishes often come from pickled and fermented ingredients, aromatic spices, fungi, and seaweeds. A wide variety of nuts, seeds, and legumes provide the necessary proteins. Tofu and seitan products also often show up in main dishes, and they are oh-so-delicious.

Vegan Chinese food culture preceded the adoption of Buddhism, but Buddhism helped to promote the vegan way of eating. Buddhism goes beyond a religion in Chinese culture. Through over a thousand years of development, it has been integrated into people's lives in the forms of foods, holidays, and customs. These are all interconnected with one another, as you will see in many recipes in this book. It's worth noting that in addition to animal products, the classic Chinese Buddhist diet also excludes everything in the onion family, such as onions, garlic, scallions, and chives.

Equipment

Here you will find a list of essential tools used in the Chinese kitchen. Once you understand what these tools are used for, you can decide whether you want to invest in them or find alternatives.

CLEAVER/OTHER KNIVES

When I was growing up, my family had two cleavers, a heavier one for cutting meats and a lighter one for cutting vegetables, which prevented cross contamination. Traditional Chinese families often don't own knives other than cleavers. That said, cleavers are really only necessary for chopping through bones. Modern chef's knives can be used in place of a cleaver for most tasks. When it comes to vegan cooking, you may use a veggie cleaver, but it is not at all mandatory. Personally, I used an 8-inch chef's knife for the dishes in this cookbook. It is lighter to handle, and you can use the flat side to smack ingredients such as ginger, garlic, and cucumbers (a common Chinese technique) just as you'd do with a cleaver.

CUTTING BOARD

Traditionally, Chinese families use a thick piece of tree trunk as a cutting board. Tree trunk cutting boards go perfectly with cleavers for heavy-duty chopping. You can use any regular cutting board for cutting vegetables and tofu with a chef's knife. Many Chinese families also have a large rectangular thin wooden cutting board to provide ample working surface for making flour-based foods such as dumplings, pancakes, and fresh noodles.

STEAMER

Steamed dishes are very common in Chinese cooking. I highly recommend having a good steamer to make some of the most authentic recipes in this book. You can use a stainless steel steamer pot (either single- or multitiered) or you can put a separate steamer basket or tray inside of or on top of a large pot. You can also use a bamboo steamer basket (either single- or multilevel) on top of a pot or wok. Whichever option you choose, make sure you have plenty of flat surface inside your steamer so you can make dumplings and rolls. Multilevel steamers are great for this. If you choose a bamboo steamer basket, I recommend one that's at least 10 inches in diameter.

WOK

Woks are ideal for making stir-fries, as you can flip the ingredients much more easily without losing them over the side. It's also common to pour liquid condiments, such as soy sauce and black vinegar, along the perimeter of the wok, around the foods, and let them slide down the curved side of the wok. The heat from the wok caramelizes the condiments and brings out more intense flavors. You can also use a wok for deep-frying and as the base for bamboo steamer baskets. Another benefit of a wok is that it heats up fast and is great at distributing heat into your foods.

Although woks come in a range of sizes, each family usually needs only one. For home use, I recommend getting one between 12 and 16 inches in diameter—a 14-inch wok is ideal, in my opinion. Woks come with either a round or a flat bottom, with flat-bottomed woks being more compatible with North American stovetops. If you buy a round-bottomed wok, make sure you also get a wok stand to accommodate it.

Typically, woks are made of cast iron, carbon steel, stainless steel, or a nonstick coating. Cast iron is very heavy; stainless steel will stick, depending on what you cook in it; and nonstick is the least healthy. I would recommend getting a carbon steel wok, because it's healthy, lighter to handle, and naturally nonstick when properly seasoned. Both cast-iron and carbon steel woks need to be seasoned (see Your Wok: Seasoning and Upkeep, page 4) to achieve a naturally nonstick surface.

You can also make all the dishes in this book without a wok, using a large stainless steel skillet, a large cast-iron skillet, or a large nonstick skillet instead, depending on what you're making. These alternative pans may not heat up as fast or provide as large a heated surface as a wok, so you will need to adjust cooking times accordingly.

Your Wok: Seasoning and Upkeep

Cast-iron and carbon steel woks need to be seasoned to build up a non-stick patina:

1. Prepare the wok by washing it with soapy water, then heat it over high heat on the stove to dry completely.
2. Use a paper towel to wipe a high-smoke-point oil—such as canola oil, vegetable oil, or avocado oil—all over the inside and outside surface of the wok. Heat the wok until the oil no longer smokes.
3. Repeat this process with a second layer of oil.

After your wok is seasoned, you should never wash it with dish soap. Wash it with hot water after each use and heat it on the stove to dry completely. If your foods start to stick in the wok, it's time to season it again.

WOK LADLE, SPATULA, SPIDER STRAINER, WOK LID

There are some cooking utensils and accessories that are designed specifically for wok cooking: A **wok spatula** is a must for stir-frying, because it has the best shape for flipping and stirring ingredients. A **wok ladle** is useful for scooping and pouring liquid ingredients, such as oil, water, and soy sauce. A mesh **spider strainer** is used to remove deep-fried items from oil or blanched foods from boiling water. If you would like to use your wok to cook braised dishes and stews, you'll also need to buy a **wok lid**.

CHOPSTICKS

Chopsticks are a very useful cooking tool. I like to use chopsticks to stir noodles, flip shallow-fried items, and pick deep-fried items out of hot oil. I would recommend getting a pair of long bamboo cooking chopsticks instead of using painted eating chopsticks.

ROLLING PIN

Chinese rolling pins, which are used for making dumpling wrappers, pancakes, and other flour-based foods, are lightweight. For regular home use, all you need is a skinny one that is 1 to 1¼ inches thick and 12 inches long; they taper a little bit at the ends.

RICE COOKER

A rice cooker is an essential tool in every modern Chinese kitchen. In addition to cooking rice flawlessly, rice cookers often come with preprogrammed functions to distinguish between white rice, brown rice, and porridge or congee, as well as timer features. Personally, I use the 5½-cup model made by the Japanese brand Zojirushi, which is extremely well made.

PRESSURE COOKER

Almost every Chinese family owns a pressure cooker. They can be used to speed up the cooking time of beans and legumes (which are staple items in the vegan Chinese diet). I grew up with old-fashioned pressure cookers at home, designed for the stovetop; now I use an Instant Pot, which has all the pressure cooking features and is more convenient and safer to handle. While I don't include pressure cooker instructions in the recipes here, you can use one to speed up the cooking time for any recipe that calls for dried beans, such as the Mixed Bean Rice (page 71) and the Eight Treasure Congee (page 81).

Cooking Skills

As you are cooking through this book, you will come across some techniques you may not be familiar with. This section will help you master the most common Chinese cooking skills.

KNIFE TECHNIQUES

Slice: This is a common technique for cutting long cylinder-shaped vegetables, such as carrots and cucumbers. Slice perpendicularly into the ingredient with your knife to create rounds or at an angle (diagonally) to produce longer ovals. If the object is too large, you can split it in half lengthwise first and then slice it into half-moons.

Julienne: Once an ingredient has been cut into slices, stack the slices like fallen dominos and cut them into matchsticks. The spacing between cuts should match the thickness of the slices, so you end up with even strips with the same thickness in both dimensions.

Dice/cube: Cut the ingredient into slices, then cut the slices into strips the same dimension as the thickness of the slice. Rotate the knife 90 degrees to the direction of the strips and cut the strips into cubes. The thickness of the slices determines the size of your cubes.

Angle-cut: Create thin, angled slices by holding the blade of the knife at a low angle to the cutting board as you cut. (This is usually used to thinly slice celery or the sturdier parts of ingredients such as the ribs of cabbage or bottoms of bok choy.)

Roll-cut (oblique-cut): In this technique, the ingredient is first cut at an oblique angle, somewhere between 45 and 60 degrees. Then, using your other hand, you roll the ingredient over 90 to 180 degrees and make another diagonal cut. This diagonal cutting and rolling will result in a piece whose two sides have different angles (not parallel to one another). You then continue this process for the length of the ingredient. You might have to split larger (wider) vegetables lengthwise into halves or quarters before you can roll-cut them.

Mincing garlic or ginger: Use the flat side of your chef's knife or cleaver to smash the ingredient with force. Then slice the ingredient. Lastly, turn the ingredients 90 degrees and chop them again to produce a mince.

Slicing scallions: Split the scallion stalk in half lengthwise, then slice it crosswise into small half-moons about ⅛ inch thick. (In most Chinese cooking, both the white and green parts of the stalk are used.)

Using a Cleaver

Chinese vegetable cleavers, sometimes called a Chinese chef's knife, are lightweight. (There are also Chinese meat cleavers, which are thicker and heavier and are meant for chopping through poultry bones, as well as ribs and cartilage.) When using a vegetable cleaver to cut vegetables, anchor the top corner of the blade on the cutting board, then rock the cleaver up and down on the curved blade. This movement can cut vegetables quickly. Cleavers have a large side surface that is also useful for smacking vegetables and is good for scooping up chopped ingredients and transferring them to the wok or another container.

FOLDING DUMPLINGS

To make dumplings, place 1½ to 2 teaspoons of filling in the center of a dumpling wrapper. If you are using store-bought wrappers, apply some water to the edges of the wrapper to make it sticky (but don't get it too wet).

Simple Dumpling Fold

For beginners, fold the wrapper in half and seal the edge, then use your fingers to make small pleats along the edge from one end to the other (as illustrated). Place the dumpling on a large plate or baking sheet dusted with flour to prevent it from sticking to the surface and repeat the process with the remaining wrappers and filling. This is the method we teach kids; keep in mind that dumplings made this way will not sit up on a plate.

Pleated Crescent Fold

As you get more advanced, you can learn to make the pleated crescent fold, which gives the dumplings a crescent curve, allowing them to sit up. To do this, fold the wrapper in half to make a half-moon shape, then pinch the middle spot of the half-moon to seal just that middle spot. Starting from one end of the half-moon, about one-third of the way from the end on the side closer to you, pinch the wrapper together, leaving more wrapper on the back side than the front. Pinch the same spot on the other side of the half-moon. Then, working toward the middle, pleat the back side of the wrapper to close the dumpling. The finished dumpling will be curved forward in a crescent and able to sit up on a flat surface.

Folding Wontons

To fold wontons, lay a square wonton wrapper on a clean work surface and place 1 teaspoon of filling in the center. Dip the tip of your fingers in a small bowl of water and moisten the edge of the wrapper along all four sides. Bring the opposite corners together to form a triangle and press the edges to seal. Bring the two bottom corners together, crisscrossing their ends. Pinch the ends together to seal, moistening the edges of the wrapper as needed to help them stick together. Place the finished wontons on a large plate or baking sheet dusted with flour and repeat with the remaining wrappers and filling.

FRYING AND STIR-FRYING

Recipes in this book make use of shallow-frying, deep-frying, and stir-frying techniques. When you're shallow-frying, the ingredient is touching the bottom of the skillet and is only cooked in a small amount of oil. When you're deep-frying, the ingredient needs to be cooked in a sufficient amount of oil that it can float on the oil's surface. Stir-frying is a common Chinese cooking technique that uses a small amount of oil but involves very high heat and fast cooking. To stir-fry, use a wok spatula to flip the ingredients constantly and vigorously. Alternatively, you can toss the ingredients by shaking the wok (though this is trickier and your ingredients may jump out of the pan).

STEAMING

Steaming is a common Chinese cooking technique and one of the healthiest possible cooking methods. Steaming is often used to cook dumplings, rolls, buns, and vegetables. Depending on the dish you are making, you can steam the food in a dish placed inside the steamer or place the food directly into the steamer basket or tray. If you're placing the food directly into the steamer, you'll need to line the steamer with cabbage leaves or a piece of parchment paper to prevent your food from sticking to the steamer. If you are steaming an item that isn't sticky and you want more steam to come through, you can line the steamer with cheesecloth instead.

Common Ingredients

PANTRY STAPLES

These ingredients form the foundation of a vegan Chinese kitchen. Most are inexpensive with a long shelf life, so it's easy to stock up. You can get them from Chinese supermarkets or order them online.

Cooking oil: Chinese cooking typically uses peanut oil, soybean oil, sunflower oil, corn oil, or canola oil. For a healthier alternative, I use avocado oil. For the recipes in this book, I chose canola oil as it's the most available in North America, but you can use any of these cooking oils interchangeably unless otherwise specified. I usually avoid oils with distinctive flavors that may interfere with the flavors of Chinese cooking, such as olive oil and coconut oil.

Sesame oil: 100-percent pure toasted sesame oil has a dark amber color. If possible, sesame oil should not be used for high-heat cooking. Best to add it to salads or use it as the finishing touch on a cooked dish.

Chili oil: This is a staple ingredient in Sichuan cuisine and in many spicy dishes. There are a variety of chili oil products incorporating different flavors in Chinese supermarkets. A basic chili oil that consists of oil, chili powder, chili flakes, and (often) sesame seeds is the most versatile for cooking the dishes in this book. If you want a wider variety of flavors, try the Lao Gan Ma brand, which has great products. Or you can make your own basic and versatile Sichuan Chili Oil (page 110).

White rice vinegar: This vinegar is pale yellow and has a light taste. It is gluten-free.

Black vinegar: This is the most frequently used vinegar in Chinese cooking and gives many dishes their distinctive flavor. There are a variety of regional vinegars all made from a combination of grains, such as rice, wheat, sorghum, barley, and peas, so black vinegar is not gluten-free. The most well-known kinds are Chinkiang vinegar and Shanxi superior mature (or extra-aged) vinegar.

Rice wine: There are a wide variety of Chinese rice wines made in different regions of the country. The amber-colored Shaoxing wine is the most well known and is what I used for the recipes in this book. In the absence of Shaoxing wine, you can use any kind of Chinese rice wine intended for cooking.

Soy sauce: When Chinese people say soy sauce, they're typically referring to light soy sauce, which adds flavor to many Chinese dishes. (The "light" is a reference to the color of the soy sauce and does not indicate that it is light in sodium—in fact it is higher in sodium than other soy sauces.) Dark soy sauce has a molasses undertone and is typically only used to enhance color. Neither light nor dark soy sauces are gluten-free. For a gluten-free substitute, use gluten-free soy sauce or tamari.

Vegetarian oyster sauce: Vegetarian oyster sauce mimics regular oyster sauce by using mushroom powder instead of oyster extract. This is a thick sauce that adds umami and is often used in Cantonese cooking.

Fermented black beans: Fermented whole black soybeans are usually packed in oil. They add a strong, salty, umami flavor to stir-fries and braised dishes.

Doubanjiang (fermented chili bean paste): This ingredient, made from broad beans (aka fava beans) and chilis, is primarily used in Sichuan cuisine. It has a chunky texture and adds a salty and spicy flavor to dishes. The most famous kind is pi xian doubanjiang, which has a deep-red color from a long fermentation.

Tianmian sauce: Also known as sweet bean sauce or sweet flour sauce, this fermented mix of wheat flour and soybeans is slightly sweet with a punch of umami. It is served with Peking duck and used for making fried sauce noodles. It's also great as a dip for raw vegetables or as a flavoring ingredient in stir-fries.

Yellow soybean paste: This fermented soybean paste from northern China is dark brown and has a strong, salty flavor. Its most popular use is in fried sauce noodles, but it can also be used in stir-fries. Although this can come as a dry paste, it's easier to use when it comes as a sauce, which is what I used for developing the recipes in this book.

Chinese sesame paste: This thick paste is made from white sesame seeds. If the oil and solids separate, simply stir them back together.

Sesame seeds: Toasted sesame seeds are often added to dishes as garnish. If only raw sesame seeds are available, toast them in a dry skillet over medium-low heat for 5 to 7 minutes, stirring constantly, until they are fragrant and slightly golden.

Five-spice powder: This mix of five (or more) ground spices usually contains Sichuan peppercorns, star anise, cinnamon, cloves, and fennel seeds.

Star anise: This star-shaped spice is often used in stews and braised dishes.

Bay leaves: These fragrant leaves are often used in stews and pickling brines.

Cinnamon sticks: Chinese cooking uses cassia (as opposed to Ceylon cinnamon), the same type that is widely available in North America.

Cumin: Cumin is an important ingredient in western China. You can buy whole seeds or ground cumin.

Ground white pepper: Most Chinese recipes call for ground white pepper, instead of ground black pepper, for its milder flavor.

Red Sichuan peppercorns: Red Sichuan peppercorns have a citrusy flavor and give dishes a distinctive numbing sensation. You can buy whole seed pods or powder; the recipes in this book use both. I prefer to grind my own peppercorn powder, as it loses flavor quickly.

Dried red chili peppers: The most common chili in Chinese markets is the facing heaven chili pepper. These small, flat chilies have moderate heat.

Dried shiitake mushrooms: These umami-filled mushrooms are essential in vegan cooking. Dried shiitake mushrooms come in different sizes, but you can use any of them. For recipes in this book, assume medium-size shiitake mushrooms (weighing about 2.5g each). If you are using smaller or larger ones, adjust the recipe accordingly.

Dried lily flowers: Considered a vegetable in Chinese cooking, dried lily flowers are frequently used in vegan and Buddhist dishes.

Dried wood ear mushrooms: Wood ear mushrooms (also known as black fungus) are a great source of protein, fiber, and micronutrients. They are widely used in Chinese cooking and are integral to vegan dishes.

Snow fungus: This widely used fungus (also known as white fungus) is a nutritious health food and is often used in Chinese food-therapy dishes.

Goji berries: These little red berries are great for general immune support, strengthening liver and kidney function, and protecting eyesight. They are frequently used in soups and teas as a medicinal ingredient.

Jujubes: Also known as Chinese red dates, these sweet dried fruits are considered a superfood that supports the immune system.

Lotus seeds: These large, white seeds are highly nutritious and frequently used in food-therapy recipes like soups and congee.

Dried lily bulbs: These dried creamy-white scales (which look like curved flower petals) come from the bulbs of a lily plant. They are often used in food-therapy dishes to calm coughs.

Rock sugar: Rock sugar is a crystallized sugar frequently used in Chinese cooking. If you can't find rock sugar, substitute a light-colored sugar of your choice.

Brown sugar: Chinese brown sugar is called "red sugar." It has a dark brown color and a deeper flavor than white sugar. Another similar ingredient is called "black sugar" in Chinese markets. For the recipes in this book, you can use either or substitute a generic brown sugar.

Zha cai (pickled mustard stems): These preserved mustard stems are julienned and sold in vacuum-sealed packages. The most popular brand (and the one I use in my kitchen) is Yuquan Zhacai.

Sui mi ya cai (preserved mustard greens): This product is sold in vacuum-sealed packages. Preserved mustard greens are triple-fermented and very flavorful. *Sui mi* in the name means the mustard greens in the package are finely chopped.

Canned vegetables: Buddhist-style vegan dishes often call for baby corn, straw mushrooms, and bamboo shoots. These ingredients are hard to find fresh, so it's best to have some canned versions on hand.

Rice: Chinese cooks use a wide variety of rice. For the recipes in this book, I used medium-grain white rice, medium-grain brown rice, black rice (often sold under the trade name Forbidden Rice), and white glutinous rice, which can also be called sticky rice or sweet rice.

Beans: Beans are often used in both sweet and savory dishes in Chinese cooking. For the recipes in this book, I used black-eyed peas, red beans (adzuki beans), mung beans, and yellow soybeans.

Other grains: Chinese dishes incorporate a wide variety of grains. I have used millet and cornmeal in the recipes in this book. When buying millet, make sure to buy a Chinese millet, which has a different taste and texture than the varieties from other countries.

Wheat noodles: In China, fresh wheat noodles are easily accessible. In North America, dried wheat noodles are much easier to find, and they last a long time in storage. Wheat noodles can be round or flat and come in a range of thicknesses.

Rice noodles: While wheat noodles are popular in northern China, rice noodles are popular in southern China. Rice noodles can be used the same way as wheat noodles but are gluten-free. In this book, I use a thin rice noodle, known as rice vermicelli.

Glass noodles: Called fensi in Chinese, these thin white noodles are made from mung bean starch. The best-known kind is Longkou vermicelli. Once cooked, they become semitranslucent.

Wonton wrappers / spring roll wrappers: You can find wonton wrappers in the refrigerated section of Chinese markets and spring roll wrappers in the freezer section. Spring roll wrappers (or spring roll pastry) are wheat-based and shouldn't be confused with the Vietnamese rice paper wrappers in the dried ingredient section. I use Home Spring brand for spring roll wrappers.

Glutinous rice flour: This is often used in desserts to create a sticky, gluten-free dough. Be careful not to confuse glutinous rice flour with regular rice flour. Glutinous rice is sometimes called sticky rice or sweet rice.

Cornstarch: This is typically used as a thickener or to produce a crispy outer crust on fried dishes. You can use potato starch or tapioca starch instead of cornstarch, but when using them as a thickener, keep in mind that each one reacts differently when subjected to heat, so you will need to adjust the amount of starch and it's cooking time accordingly.

Gypsum: Gypsum, or calcium sulfate, is used as a coagulant to make tofu. You can buy gypsum from brewing supply stores, as it's also used to brew beer.

Active dry yeast: This common yeast is used to leaven breads and rolls in Chinese cooking. Angel brand is the yeast I used in the recipes in this book.

Vital wheat gluten: This is the base ingredient for making seitan products. You can find it at health food stores.

TOFU AND SEITAN

Tofu and seitan make tasty and substantial meat replacements. Both originated in China, and they are at the center of many vegan dinner tables. You will find a variety of tofu and seitan products in Chinese supermarkets. Here are some of the ones that appear in the recipes in this book:

Fresh tofu: Tofu is made from coagulated soy milk whose curds are then pressed into a block. Depending on how much water is pressed out of the tofu curd, the block can have a soft, medium, firm, or extra-firm texture. It's surprisingly easy to make your own Tofu from Scratch (page 107) as well.

Dried tofu: Although this product is called "dried" tofu, it isn't actually dehydrated. Instead, it is fresh tofu that has had even more liquid pressed out of it. It is also known as "pressed" tofu. This is sometimes marinated to give it a five-spice flavor, and I use this version in my recipes. You will find dried tofu in vacuum-sealed packages in the refrigerated section of Chinese markets.

Fresh bean curd sheets: This tofu is pressed into sheets instead of blocks. You can cut it into small squares to use as a wrapper (like a tortilla) or into strips to make salads, and it is the main ingredient in Mock Meat (page 109). It is sold in the refrigerated section of Chinese markets.

Tofu puffs: Tofu puffs—deep-fried tofu cubes—are often used in stir-fries, stews, and soups. You can make your own Tofu Puffs (page 108), but the kind you find in the refrigerated section of Chinese markets are made from a special kind of tofu and have a puffy texture.

Tofu skin: This ingredient (also known as bean curd skin or yuba) is made by pulling off the skin that forms when you heat soy milk. It is sold in the freezer section of the Chinese supermarket and may be labeled "frozen bean curd sheet." It needs to be thawed before use. This is the main ingredient in the recipe for Bean Curd Rolls (page 96). These thin sheets are bendable once thawed and should not be confused with the thicker, stiffer dried bean curd sheets found in the dried ingredient section. The ones I use come as large round sheets about 26 inches in diameter. You can also buy half-round sheets; if you do, you can mix flour and water to make a paste and glue them together into a full round or use them as is to make smaller rolls. The rectangular tofu skins work just the same.

Dried bean curd sticks: These long, dense "sticks," called fu zhu in Chinese, are made from bean curd skin that is hung to dry in a bunch after it is taken out of boiling soy milk. They have a meaty texture and are often used in stir-fries, soups, stews, and braised dishes.

Fried gluten balls: These delicious, puffy balls, or mian jin in Chinese, are made by deep-frying small balls of gluten dough. You can make Fried Gluten Balls (page 105) at home or find them in the refrigerated section of Chinese markets. In vegan dishes, fried gluten balls add flavor and substance in soups, stews, and braised dishes.

Steamed seitan (kao fu): This is a steamed leavened gluten bread that is always cut into cubes. You can easily make Steamed Seitan (page 104) from scratch or find it in the refrigerated section of Chinese markets.

A Short Guide to Mock Meats

Legend has it that mock meats were originally created in Buddhist monasteries to entertain outside guests and satisfy the monks who ate a boring and bland diet. Vegan Chinese cooks use a wide variety of mock meats. The most common ready-made packaged mock meats sold in Chinese markets are traditional bean curd products, some of which have been made since 500 CE. These mock meats may be labeled "vegetarian chicken," "vegetarian duck," or "vegetarian goose" and are made by boiling fresh bean curd sheets in a marinade, then rolling and pressing them. Some are smoked, and others are flavored with a variety of spices—I encourage you to try them all! Simply cut them into slices and serve them cold or reheated with your favorite dipping sauce, or toss them in a salad. If you'd like to make your own, try the Mock Meat (page 109) recipe. In regions near Shanghai, homemade vegetarian duck and goose are stuffed with vegetables and then panfried until crispy. See the Bean Curd Rolls (page 96) for my take on this delightful treat. These days, Chinese cooks may also use newer mock meat options, including some that use gluten and/or vegetables to imitate the shape and taste of seafood and meat products.

FRESH VEGETABLES

The recipes in this book use a wide variety of different vegetables, including some traditional Chinese types that are less common in supermarkets but are readily available in Chinatowns and Asian markets:

Garlic: This is an important ingredient in Chinese cooking, frequently used in salads, stir-fries, braised dishes, and dipping sauces.

Ginger: Aromatic ginger is used in a variety of dishes. To peel ginger, use a small paring knife or spoon to gently scrape off the skin.

Onions: Chinese cooks use green onions (aka scallions), yellow onions, red onions, and shallots. The green onions in China are very large, about the size of a leek. For the recipes in this book, I used the smaller scallions common in North America. Whenever scallions are called for, you should use both the white and green parts of the stalk.

Long hot peppers: Also known as Italian long hots, these chilies are green when they are young and turn red when they mature. The green ones are used as a vegetable—some are mild and some are spicy, and you never know what you're going to get. The red ones add heat to dishes.

English cucumbers: Chinese cucumbers are smaller and crunchier than English cucumbers, but they're hard to find. I've used the large English cucumbers commonly found in supermarkets for the recipes in this book.

Fresh mushrooms: Mushrooms are often the star ingredient in vegan dishes. The most-used mushrooms in Chinese cooking (and in this book) are oyster mushrooms, king oyster mushrooms (also known as king trumpet mushrooms), and enoki mushrooms.

Chinese eggplant: These long, thin eggplants have relatively thin skin and are very tender. They are ideal for stir-fries and braising, but you can substitute globe eggplants if needed.

Bean sprouts: There are two common kinds of bean sprouts: soybean sprouts and mung bean sprouts. Soybean sprouts are thicker with larger yellow heads; mung bean sprouts are more tender and often have the green outer skin of the mung bean on their heads. You can use either in the recipes in this book, though I prefer mung bean sprouts and that is what I used in creating these recipes.

Bok choy: This leafy green vegetable is a type of Chinese cabbage and comes in a whole range of sizes. Baby bok choy can be as small as 3 to 4 inches, while full-size bok choy grows up to 18 inches in average length. I use both in this book.

Chinese broccoli: Known as gai lan in Chinese, this long leafy vegetable is very tasty. It is similar to broccolini, but it has leaves instead of florets.

Yu choy: This stalky vegetable looks like Chinese broccoli but is more tender.

Mustard greens: Called gai choy in Cantonese or jie cai in Mandarin, this green vegetable is often pickled. It's also surprisingly delicious when cooked fresh.

Napa cabbage: This popular Chinese cabbage is sweet and tender and is a staple winter vegetable in northern China. When I was a child, many families stored over 100 pounds of napa cabbage in their homes during the winter.

Taiwanese flat cabbage: This flat cabbage is very similar to the regular green cabbage you see in North American supermarkets, but it is larger, juicier, and more tender. You can substitute regular cabbage, but if you can find Taiwanese flat cabbage, you may want to use them in all your cabbage dishes (even the non-Chinese ones).

Daikon: This large white radish is another winter staple in China. Daikon can be pickled, braised, or stewed. It is often eaten to calm coughs and nourish the lungs.

About the Recipes

You will find a variety of classic vegan Chinese recipes in this cookbook. I tried to keep these well-known dishes as authentic as possible, which means you may see a few ingredients you aren't familiar with and a slightly longer ingredient list. Please trust me that it will be worthwhile to make these authentic flavors at home. At the same time, I tried to keep the workflow as straightforward as possible so that these dishes are approachable for North American cooks. Among this collection, I included a good number of easy recipes with shorter ingredient lists for busy families. These recipes are still authentic, and they are popular homestyle dishes because they are quick and extremely flavorful. You will also find some restaurant favorites common here in North America.

Silken Tofu Salad, PAGE 31

2

Salads and Cold Appetizers

拍黄瓜 SMACKED CUCUMBER SALAD

I'll go out on a limb and say that this dish is the most popular cold appetizer dish on Chinese tables, both at restaurants and at home. Smacking the cucumber with the side of the knife breaks down its fibers and helps it soak up the garlicky spicy-sour dressing. This bold and refreshing salad will surely whet your appetite.

PREP TIME:
10 minutes, plus
20 minutes to rest

2 large English cucumbers

1 tablespoon sea salt

4 garlic cloves, minced

3 tablespoons black vinegar

2 teaspoons Chinese light soy sauce

2 teaspoons sesame oil

1½ teaspoons granulated sugar

1 tablespoon Sichuan Chili Oil (page 110) or store-bought chili oil

½ cup fresh cilantro, cut into 2-inch lengths

1. Trim the ends off the cucumbers and lay them on a cutting board. Smack the cucumbers firmly with the flat side of a chef's knife, working from one end of the cucumber to the other, until the cucumbers crack. Split the smacked cucumbers in half lengthwise. Lay each half flat-side up. Cut the cucumbers diagonally into ½-inch-thick, 2-inch-long slices.

2. In a medium bowl, toss the cucumber and salt together until thoroughly combined and let them rest for 20 minutes.

3. Squeeze out as much juice as possible from the cucumber (discard the cucumber juice). Transfer the cucumber to a clean medium bowl.

4. Add the garlic, vinegar, soy sauce, sesame oil, sugar, chili oil, and cilantro to the bowl. Mix everything together.

5. For the best flavor, refrigerate the salad until you serve it.

PREP TIP: This is a salad you can make a few hours ahead of time for dinner parties, barbecues, potlucks, and picnics. The flavor only gets better as the cucumbers absorb the dressing. Make sure to keep the salad chilled in the meantime.

PER SERVING: Calories: 84; Total fat: 5g; Saturated fat: 0.5g; Carbohydrates: 6g; Sugar: 4g; Protein: 2g; Calcium: 42mg

大拌菜 MIXED RAINBOW VEGETABLE SALAD

This modern mixed vegetable salad (da ban cai) is popular on restaurant menus in China. The dressing is made with traditional Chinese ingredients, but the presentation is Westernized by using a mix of colorful and nutritious raw ingredients often seen in American-style salads. Here is my take on this popular fusion salad.

PREP TIME:
10 minutes

- **3 cups lightly packed frisée, cut into 2-inch segments**
- **1/2 red bell pepper, cut into bite-size pieces**
- **1/2 yellow bell pepper, cut into bite-size pieces**
- **1 cup (1 3/4 oz / 50g) lightly packed bite-size pieces red cabbage**
- **6 red radishes, thinly sliced**
- **1/4 large English cucumber, thinly sliced**
- **1/4 cup white rice vinegar**
- **2 tablespoons Chinese light soy sauce**
- **1 tablespoon vegetarian oyster sauce**
- **1 tablespoon granulated sugar**
- **1/2 teaspoon sea salt**
- **1 teaspoon sesame oil**
- **1/4 cup roasted peanuts (any papery skins removed)**

1. In a large salad bowl, combine the frisée, bell pepper, cabbage, radish, and cucumber.

2. In a small bowl, mix the rice vinegar, soy sauce, vegetarian oyster sauce, sugar, salt, and sesame oil together. Stir with chopsticks to dissolve the sugar and salt.

3. Add the peanuts to the vegetables. Pour the dressing into the bowl. Mix together and serve immediately.

VARIATION: This is a very flexible recipe; feel free to swap for any vegetables suitable for a raw salad.

PER SERVING: Calories: 117; Total fat: 6g; Saturated fat: 1g; Carbohydrates: 18g; Sugar: 11g; Protein: 4g; Calcium: 51mg

凉拌黑木耳 WOOD EAR MUSHROOM SALAD

This is a popular salad on restaurant menus in China, and it has a more delicious, nuanced flavor than you might expect from the ingredients. Wood ear mushrooms have a meaty texture, and in this dish they are only cooked for a short time so that they remain a little bit crunchy. They are then dressed with a savory, flavorful dressing that includes umami flavors from the soy sauce and spiciness from the red onion, garlic, and bird's eye chili.

PREP TIME: 10 minutes, plus 2 to 4 hours to rehydrate

COOK TIME: 5 minutes

- 3/4 cup (3/4 oz / 21g) dried wood ear mushrooms, soaked in cool water for 2 to 4 hours
- 1/4 cup thinly sliced red onion
- 1 fresh bird's eye chili, sliced into thin rings
- 2 garlic cloves, minced
- 2 tablespoons Chinese light soy sauce
- 1 tablespoon black vinegar
- 1 teaspoon sesame oil
- 3/4 teaspoon granulated sugar
- 1/3 cup roughly chopped fresh cilantro

1. Set up a bowl of cold water. Bring a medium pot of water to a boil over high heat. Rinse the soaked wood ears and discard the tough roots. Add the mushrooms to the boiling water and cook for 5 minutes. Transfer the mushrooms to the cold water to cool, then drain thoroughly.

2. Using your hands, tear the larger pieces of mushrooms into bite-size pieces.

3. In a medium bowl, combine the wood ears, onion, chili, garlic, soy sauce, vinegar, sesame oil, sugar, and cilantro. For the best flavor, refrigerate the salad until you serve it.

PER SERVING: Calories: 44; Total fat: 1g; Saturated fat: 0g; Carbohydrates: 7g; Sugar: 1.5g; Protein: 1g; Calcium: 24mg

凉拌菠菜粉丝 SPINACH AND GLASS NOODLE SALAD

This simple salad is tasty, refreshing, and extremely easy to make. Spinach and glass noodles are a common pairing in Chinese salads. Although there are many ways to make this dish, this recipe showcases the version from Shaanxi, where cooks frequently use hot oil to extract the fragrance of spices and herbs.

PREP TIME:
10 minutes,
plus
15 minutes to
rehydrate

COOK TIME:
10 minutes

1 (1½ oz / 40g) bunch glass noodles, soaked in cool water for 15 minutes

12 cups (14oz / 400g) lightly packed spinach, cut into 2-inch-long pieces

1 tablespoon black vinegar

1 teaspoon Chinese light soy sauce

½ teaspoon sea salt

½ teaspoon granulated sugar

3 garlic cloves, minced

3 tablespoons canola oil

1 tablespoon red Sichuan peppercorns

3 dried red facing heaven chili peppers, cut into ¼-inch segments

1. Set up two bowls of cold water. Bring a pot of water to a boil over high heat. Add the noodles and blanch for 4 minutes, then scoop them out of the water (without draining the pot) and transfer them to one of the bowls of cold water to cool. In the same pot, blanch the spinach for 1½ minutes. Drain the spinach and transfer it to the second bowl of cold water to cool.

2. Drain the glass noodles, then use a pair of scissors to cut them into 6-inch-long pieces. Drain the spinach in a colander, then squeeze out as much water as possible.

3. In a medium bowl, combine the noodles, vinegar, soy sauce, salt, and sugar. Put the spinach on top of the noodles and pile the garlic on top.

4. In a wok, heat the oil, Sichuan peppercorns, and chilies over medium heat for 2 minutes, or until the spices are browned and the oil begins to smoke. Discard the chilies and peppercorns and immediately pour the hot oil over the garlic in the bowl.

5. Mix all the ingredients together. Serve as an appetizer or side dish.

PER SERVING: Calories: 162; Total fat: 10g; Saturated fat: 1g; Carbohydrates: 14g; Sugar: 0.5g; Protein: 2g; Calcium: 100mg

素什锦 ASSORTED VEGETARIAN DELICACIES

This dish is popular across China and has many names and variations. In my hometown, Beijing, it is called su shi jin (the name I've used here). All the ingredients are braised and then chilled, and the dish is served as a cold appetizer or side dish. The dish is even better if allowed to marinate overnight.

PREP TIME:
10 minutes, plus 8 to 16 hours to soak and to marinate

COOK TIME:
20 minutes

8 medium dried shiitake mushrooms (3/4 oz / 20g), soaked in cool water for 2 hours or up to overnight

1/3 cup (1/3 oz / 9g) dried wood ear mushrooms, soaked in cool water for 2 to 4 hours

1/2 cup (3/4 oz / 20g) dried lily flowers, soaked in warm water for 30 minutes

1 or 2 dried bean curd sticks (1oz / 30g), soaked in cool water for 4 to 6 hours

1 cup water

3 tablespoons granulated sugar

2 tablespoons Chinese light soy sauce

1 tablespoon dark soy sauce

1 teaspoon sea salt

4 tablespoons canola oil, divided

2 1/2 cups (7oz / 200g) 1-inch cubed Steamed Seitan (page 104) or store-bought Chinese steamed seitan (kao fu)

2 whole star anise

1 cinnamon stick

1/2 cup roasted peanuts (any papery skins removed)

1/4 cup thinly sliced canned bamboo shoots, drained

2 tablespoons sesame oil

1. Scoop out the rehydrated shiitakes, wood ears, lily flowers, and bean curd sticks from their respective bowls. Squeeze out the water. Reserve 1 cup of the shiitake soaking water.

2. Discard the tough ends from both types of mushroom and the lily flowers. Thinly slice the shiitake and cut the bean curd sticks into 1-inch segments at an angle.

3. In a medium bowl, combine the water, shiitake soaking water, sugar, light soy sauce, dark soy sauce, and salt. Set the sauce aside.

4. In a wok or skillet with a lid, heat 2 tablespoons of canola oil over medium-high heat until hot. Add the seitan cubes and stir for 2 minutes. Remove them and set them aside on a plate, leaving any extra oil in the pan.

5. Add the remaining 2 tablespoons of canola oil to the pan, then add the shiitake, star anise, and cinnamon stick and stir for 1 minute to release the spices' fragrance. Add the wood ear mushroom, lily flowers, bean curd sticks, peanuts, and bamboo shoots and stir for 2 minutes.

6. Add the seitan and the sauce to the pan and mix. Cover the pan, reduce the heat to medium-low, and simmer everything for 15 minutes, or until most of the sauce has reduced. If there is still a lot of sauce, uncover the pan and cook for a few more minutes. Remove the mixture from the heat and drizzle it with the sesame oil.

7. Transfer the mixture to a sealed container and refrigerate it for 4 hours, or until well chilled, before eating.

PER SERVING: Calories: 326; Total fat: 21g; Saturated fat: 2.5g; Carbohydrates: 20g; Sugar: 7.5g; Protein: 15g; Calcium: 35mg

蒜泥麻酱蒸茄子
STEAMED EGGPLANT IN GARLIC-SESAME SAUCE

We had this northern-style eggplant dish a lot at home when I was a child, and the adults usually delegated tasks like stirring the sesame sauce to me. While this healthy appetizer only uses a few simple ingredients, it's anything but boring with subtle but memorable flavors. Think of it as the Chinese baba ghanoush, but even easier to make. It's great to serve alongside a main dish with strong flavors, for balance.

PREP TIME:
20 minutes, plus 10 minutes to cool

COOK TIME:
15 minutes

¼ cup distilled white vinegar

1 medium globe eggplant (1¼ lb / 567g) or 2 Italian eggplants

3 tablespoons Chinese sesame paste

3 tablespoons water

1¼ teaspoons sea salt

6 garlic cloves, peeled

2 teaspoons sesame oil

2 tablespoons chopped fresh cilantro

SPECIAL EQUIPMENT:
Flat-bottomed stainless steel or bamboo steamer with a large pot

1. Fill a large bowl halfway with water and add the white vinegar. Peel the eggplant, cut it into ½-inch-thick slices, and immediately submerge the slices in the water to prevent browning.

2. Heat a pot of water with a steamer on top over high heat. When the pot is steaming, reduce the heat to medium and place the eggplant in the steamer. Shingle the eggplant slices into the steamer, overlapping them slightly to allow steam to come in between. Steam the eggplant for 10 minutes, or until tender. Remove the eggplant from the steamer and let it cool.

3. Meanwhile, in a small bowl, combine the sesame paste, water, and salt and stir into a smooth sauce. Using a small food processor or a mortar and pestle, thoroughly mash the garlic into a paste.

4. Squeeze any excess water out of the eggplant and use your hands to pull it into small, bite-size chunks. In a medium bowl, combine the eggplant, sesame sauce, mashed garlic, sesame oil, and cilantro and stir well.

5. Serve as an appetizer or side dish.

VARIATION: If you want to add a kick to this eggplant salad, drizzle it with a dash of black vinegar and some Sichuan Chili Oil (page 110).

PER SERVING: Calories: 131; Total fat: 8.5g; Saturated fat: 1g; Carbohydrates: 12g; Sugar: 4.5g; Protein: 4g; Calcium: 136mg

煮毛豆 BOILED YOUNG SOYBEANS

In this dish, young soybeans (edamame) are boiled in an aromatic brine until they absorb the flavor of the spices and salt and become a tasty, protein-rich appetizer or snack. When I was growing up, we followed the traditional custom of eating boiled young soybeans on the day of the Mid-Autumn Festival. My mother would boil these along with whole peanuts in their shells. It isn't that easy to find whole raw peanuts here, but boiled young soybeans alone are just as authentic.

PREP TIME:
5 minutes, plus 2 hours to marinate

COOK TIME:
25 minutes

3 whole star anise

2 teaspoons red Sichuan peppercorns

3 bay leaves

1½ tablespoons sea salt

4 cups water

1 pound (454g) frozen edamame in their pods

1. In a medium pot, toast the star anise, Sichuan peppercorns, bay leaves, and salt over medium-low heat for 3 minutes, or until fragrant, stirring frequently to make sure the spices do not burn.

2. Pour the water into the pot with the spices, then bring it to a boil over high heat. Once the water has boiled, reduce the heat to medium-low and simmer the spices for 5 minutes.

3. Meanwhile, using a pair of scissors, cut off both ends of the edamame pods. (This will help the soybeans absorb flavor.) Add the soybeans to the pot, increase the heat to high, and bring the liquid to a boil again. Then reduce the heat to medium and simmer the soybeans for 4 minutes.

4. Remove the pot from the heat. Keep the soybeans in the brine to absorb its flavor while the liquid cools to room temperature. Remove the soybeans from the brine to serve.

PREP TIP: Make this dish hours in advance to allow the edamame more time to absorb flavor. You can also double the recipe and keep the extra edamame in the brine in the refrigerator. Marinated and chilled soybeans taste even better the next day.

PER SERVING: Calories: 151; Total fat: 5g; Saturated fat: 0.5g; Carbohydrates: 12g; Sugar: 1.5g; Protein: 15g; Calcium: 91mg

台式泡菜 TAIWANESE-STYLE PICKLED CABBAGE

This quick-pickled cabbage salad is an addictive appetizer—sweet and sour and crunchy. I often serve this as a refreshing side to balance a heavy meal. The dish is traditionally made with a Taiwanese flat cabbage, which is crunchier and juicier than the regular green cabbage.

PREP TIME:
10 minutes, plus
1 hour to rest and pickle

1/2 medium Taiwanese flat cabbage (1lb 12oz / 795g) or 1 small green cabbage

1 medium carrot, thinly julienned

1 tablespoon sea salt

2 fresh bird's eye chilies

1/2 cup granulated sugar

1/2 cup white rice vinegar

4 garlic cloves, sliced

1. Remove the core of the cabbage, then cut along the cabbage midribs to split the thick ribs in half. Tear the leaves into large bite-size pieces.

2. In a large bowl, toss the cabbage pieces and the carrot with the salt. Gently massage the vegetables with your hands for 2 minutes to work in the salt, then let them sit for 30 minutes.

3. Remove the seeds from the bird's eye chilies, then cut them into long, thin slices. In a small bowl, mix the chili with the sugar, rice vinegar, and garlic to make a dressing. Stir the mixture with chopsticks to dissolve the sugar.

4. Once the vegetables have released their juices, transfer the cabbage and carrots to a colander to drain, then rinse off the remaining salt. Squeeze the vegetables to remove as much liquid as possible.

5. Put the vegetables and the dressing into a large, airtight glass container. Seal the container and shake it to mix the vegetables and the dressing together. Refrigerate the mixture for at least 30 minutes.

6. Transfer your desired amount of the pickled vegetables onto a plate and serve it cold. To store the remaining pickled cabbage, leave it in the sealed container in the refrigerator for up to 1 week.

PER SERVING: Calories: 151; Total fat: 0.5g; Saturated fat: 0g; Carbohydrates: 36g; Sugar: 29g; Protein: 3g; Calcium: 221mg

酸辣萝卜 SOUR AND SPICY PICKLED DAIKON

This Sichuan-style quick pickled daikon (suan la luo bo) is a wonderful combination of sour, sweet, and spicy. It will add a crunch and a little zing to your meal. It is ready in 1 day, but it can be stored for up to 2 weeks in the refrigerator.

PREP TIME:
10 minutes,
plus 1 day and
30 minutes
to rest
and pickle

1 daikon radish (1lb 12oz /795g)

1 tablespoon sea salt

1½ cups water

1 cup distilled white vinegar

¼ cup granulated sugar

1 (1-inch) piece fresh ginger, thinly sliced

4 garlic cloves, thinly sliced

4 fresh bird's eye chilies, cut into small rings

1. Peel and cut the daikon radish into 2-inch-long strips ¼ inch thick and transfer them to a large bowl.

2. Sprinkle the salt on the daikon and use your hands to mix thoroughly. Let the daikon rest for 30 minutes.

3. In a medium bowl, mix the water, vinegar, and sugar until well combined.

4. Drain the daikon in a colander, then put it into a clean large bowl. Add the ginger, garlic, and chili and mix everything well, then transfer the mixture to a large glass jar with a lid.

5. Pour the pickling liquid into the jar, making sure it covers the daikon. Close the jar and let the daikon pickle for 1 day in the refrigerator before eating.

6. Remove some daikon from the jar and serve as an appetizer. You can keep the rest submerged in the pickling liquid and store it in the refrigerator for up to 2 weeks.

PREP TIP: It's very common to cut daikon into cubes or slices for pickling. Change it up sometimes for a different presentation. Leftover pickled ginger, garlic, and chili can be used in stir-fries to add a lot of flavor.

PER SERVING: Calories: 50; Total fat: 0g; Saturated fat: 0g; Carbohydrates: 10g; Sugar: 6g; Protein: 1g; Calcium: 59mg

凉拌嫩豆腐 SILKEN TOFU SALAD

This is a simplified version of the Shanghai-style tofu salad that people often make with century eggs on it. My vegan tofu salad uses fewer ingredients yet still captures the essence of the dish, and the silky, smooth tofu easily takes on the flavors of the dressing and the toppings. No cooking is required for this cold appetizer.

PREP TIME:
5 minutes

1 (16oz / 454g) block silken tofu or ⅔ recipe Tofu from Scratch (page 107)

3 tablespoons chopped preserved mustard stem (zha cai)

2 tablespoons sliced scallions

2 tablespoons chopped fresh cilantro

2 tablespoons Chinese light soy sauce

1 tablespoon sesame oil

2 teaspoons black vinegar

1. Drain the tofu and place it upside down on a deep plate.

2. Cut the tofu in half lengthwise, then cut it crosswise into ½-inch-thick slices, but leave the slices in the shape of the original block of tofu.

3. Sprinkle the chopped preserved mustard stem, scallion, and cilantro on top of the tofu.

4. In a small bowl, mix the soy sauce, sesame oil, and vinegar together.

5. Pour the dressing over the tofu. Serve immediately.

PREP TIP: Make sure the tofu is well drained, so that the dressing is not diluted.

INGREDIENT TIP: These preserved mustard stems are julienned and sold in vacuum-sealed packages. The most popular brand and the one I use in this recipe is labeled Yuquan Zhacai. They add great flavors to the tofu salad.

PER SERVING: Calories: 91; Total fat: 6g; Saturated fat: 0.5g; Carbohydrates: 2g; Sugar: 0.5g; Protein: 5g; Calcium: 90mg

凉拌芦笋 EASY ASPARAGUS SALAD

This is the quickest way to make a Chinese-style vegetable salad. When I am short on time at home, I simply blanch some green vegetables and then toss in this simple dressing. You can serve it as an appetizer or a cold vegetable side dish.

PREP TIME:
5 minutes

COOK TIME:
5 minutes

1 pound (454g) asparagus

1 tablespoon canola oil

1½ teaspoons sea salt, divided

2 garlic cloves, minced

1 teaspoon sesame oil

½ teaspoon toasted sesame seeds (optional)

1. Snap off the tough ends of the asparagus spears. Cut the asparagus diagonally into 2-inch-long pieces.

2. Bring a medium pot of water to a boil over high heat. Add the canola oil and 1 teaspoon of salt. Add the asparagus and blanch for about 2 minutes, or until it is just tender.

3. Drain the asparagus in a colander and let it cool to room temperature.

4. Transfer the cooled asparagus to a medium bowl and toss it with the garlic, sesame oil, and remaining ½ teaspoon of salt.

5. Sprinkle with toasted sesame seeds (if using) and serve.

VARIATION: Try this recipe with green beans, broccolini, spinach, or yu choy. Adjust the cooking time depending on the vegetable you use. If you are using a leafy vegetable, make sure to squeeze out excess water after blanching.

PER SERVING: Calories: 55; Total fat: 4.5g; Saturated fat: 0.5g; Carbohydrates: 3g; Sugar: 1g; Protein: 1g; Calcium: 17mg

乾隆白菜 QIANLONG CABBAGE

This napa cabbage salad is famous in China because legend has it that Emperor Qianlong, who brought the Qing empire to the highest prosperity, loved this dish. This tangy, sweet, and savory salad is also really easy to make. The dressing usually contains honey, but I use maple syrup to make it vegan.

PREP TIME:
15 minutes

3 tablespoons Chinese sesame paste

2 tablespoons granulated sugar

2 tablespoons black vinegar

1 teaspoon sesame oil

1/2 teaspoon dark soy sauce

1/4 teaspoon sea salt

1 tablespoon maple syrup

5 cups (9oz / 250g) tightly packed napa cabbage leaves, inner yellow leaves only (no midribs)

1 tablespoon toasted white sesame seeds, plus more for garnish

1. In a large bowl, mix the sesame paste, sugar, black vinegar, sesame oil, dark soy sauce, salt, and maple syrup together. The mixture should be thick and stick to the spoon.

2. Tear the cabbage leaves into large bite-size pieces and add them to the bowl. Mix the cabbage and the sauce together until all the leaves are coated. Mix in the sesame seeds.

3. Stack the cabbage in a small pile on a plate and garnish them with more sesame seeds. Serve immediately.

PREP TIP: Make sure the cabbage leaves are completely dry before adding them to the bowl. Any water on the cabbage leaves will dilute the sauce and keep it from sticking. If the dish is made correctly, there shouldn't be a liquid dressing pooling under the cabbage.

INGREDIENT TIP: You can use the outer cabbage leaves leftover from this dish in the Napa Cabbage, Glass Noodles, and Gluten Ball Soup (page 64). The thick napa cabbage midribs can be used in the Napa Cabbage Stir-Fry with Vinegar Sauce (page 44).

PER SERVING: Calories: 239; Total fat: 17g; Saturated fat: 2g; Carbohydrates: 17g; Sugar: 10g; Protein: 5g; Calcium: 280mg

*Sautéed Potato,
Green Peppers, and
Eggplant, PAGE 46*

3

Stir-Fries

椒盐豆腐 SALT AND PEPPER TOFU

Everyone loves this Shanghai-style crispy tofu sprinkled with a generous amount of chili and Sichuan pepper salt. This is a quick dish to make at home. The Sichuan peppercorns add a distinctive numbing kick to this spicy dish.

PREP TIME:
10 minutes

COOK TIME:
20 minutes

1½ (16oz / 454 g) blocks firm or extra-firm tofu or 1 recipe Tofu from Scratch (page 107), drained and patted dry

1½ teaspoons sea salt, divided

2 tablespoons cornstarch

1 tablespoon canola oil, plus more for deep-frying

6 fresh bird's eye chilies, cut into small rings

4 garlic cloves, minced

2 tablespoons sliced scallions

1 teaspoon red Sichuan peppercorn powder

1. Cut the tofu into ¾-inch cubes and sprinkle them with 1 teaspoon of salt. Let the tofu sit for 10 minutes.

2. Toss the tofu cubes in the cornstarch. In a deep pot, heat at least 3 inches of oil over medium-high heat. When a wooden chopstick lowered into the oil immediately sizzles, the oil is ready. Carefully drop in the cubes of tofu and fry them for 6 to 8 minutes, until the outsides are crispy and golden. Use a spider strainer or slotted spoon to remove the tofu from the oil and set it aside on a plate. (You may need to fry the tofu in batches, depending on the size of the pot.)

3. In a wok or skillet, heat 1 tablespoon of oil over medium heat. Add the chili, garlic, and scallion and stir for about 1 minute, or until fragrant. Add the Sichuan peppercorn powder and stir for 10 seconds. Add the tofu and the remaining ½ teaspoon of salt and stir for 30 seconds. Remove the pan from the heat, transfer the tofu to a serving plate, and sprinkle it with the chili-pepper-salt mixture.

4. Serve hot as part of a meal or a snack.

PER SERVING: Calories: 272; Total fat: 17g; Saturated fat: 2g; Carbohydrates: 9g; Sugar: 1g; Protein: 17g; Calcium: 139mg

左宗堂豆腐 GENERAL TSO'S TOFU

Although the original version of this dish was named after a historic figure from Hunan Province, it was invented in Taiwan in the 1950s to serve to American guests at banquets. This version is made without deep-frying.

PREP TIME:
5 minutes

COOK TIME:
25 minutes

2 (16oz / 454g) blocks firm tofu or 1¹/₃ recipes Tofu from Scratch (page 107), drained and patted dry, in 1" cubes

1 teaspoon sea salt

¹/₄ teaspoon ground white pepper

1 cup water

¹/₂ cup granulated sugar

¹/₄ cup white rice vinegar

¹/₄ cup Shaoxing wine

¹/₄ cup Chinese light soy sauce

2 tablespoons cornstarch

3 dried red facing heaven chili peppers

4 tablespoons canola oil, divided

6 garlic cloves, minced

2 teaspoons minced fresh ginger

1 teaspoon toasted white sesame seeds

1. Cut the tofu cubes in half to make each ½ inch thick; sprinkle with salt and pepper. In a medium bowl, mix the water, sugar, vinegar, rice wine, soy sauce, and cornstarch. Cut the chilies into ½-inch segments and add them to the sauce.

2. In a nonstick skillet, heat 2 tablespoons of oil over medium-high heat until hot but not smoking. Add some of the tofu in a single layer until the pan is filled, and fry for 3 to 4 minutes on each side, until crispy and golden. Transfer the tofu to a dish and set it aside. Repeat with the remaining tofu in batches.

3. Remove the pan from the heat and let it cool down slightly. Add the remaining 2 tablespoons of oil, the garlic, and ginger and cook in the residual heat until fragrant. Add the sauce to the pan, set the pan over high heat, and cook for about 2 minutes, stirring, until it boils and thickens.

4. Add the tofu and toss gently. Cook for 1 to 2 minutes, until the sauce reduces to the desired consistency. Sprinkle with sesame seeds. Serve hot.

PER SERVING: Calories: 467; Total fat: 24g; Saturated fat: 2g; Carbohydrates: 38g; Sugar: 27g; Protein: 22g; Calcium: 446mg

蒜蓉辣椒豆泡炒杂蔬
CHILI-GARLIC TOFU PUFFS AND MIXED VEGETABLES

Stir-fry with chili-garlic sauce is the dish that comes to my mind when I think of North American Chinese food. When I came to Canada 20 years ago, I was surprised to find that Chinese food here is nothing like the food back home. Nonetheless, I grew to enjoy many of the dishes I found here, including this one.

PREP TIME:
5 minutes

COOK TIME:
10 minutes

3 cups (5oz / 150g) bite-size broccoli florets

1 tablespoon cornstarch

²/₃ cup water

2 tablespoons canola oil, divided

1 small carrot, thinly sliced on the diagonal

1/2 red bell pepper, cut into 1-inch squares

10 white mushrooms, halved

6 garlic cloves, minced

4 Tofu Puffs (page 108) or store-bought tofu puffs, halved

1 tablespoon Shaoxing wine

1¹/₄ teaspoons sea salt

1 teaspoon granulated sugar

1 tablespoon Sichuan Chili Oil (page 110) or store-bought chili oil

1. Bring a medium pot of water to a boil over high heat. Add the broccoli and cook it for 1 minute, then drain the broccoli in a colander.

2. In a small bowl, mix the cornstarch and water to make a thickener and set it aside.

3. In a wok or skillet, heat 1 tablespoon of oil over high heat. Add the carrot, bell pepper, and mushroom and stir for 1 minute. Add the remaining 1 tablespoon of oil, the garlic, and tofu puffs and stir for 1 minute. Add the wine, salt, sugar, and chili oil and stir to combine.

4. Add the broccoli to the pan and stir for 2 minutes. Add the cornstarch mixture and stir for 1 minute, or until the sauce thickens. Serve hot.

PER SERVING: Calories: 200; Total fat: 14g; Saturated fat: 1g; Carbohydrates: 12g; Sugar: 4.5g; Protein: 6g; Calcium: 65mg

宫保土豆 **KUNG PAO POTATOES**

This famous sweet-and-sour dish gets its pronounced flavor from spicy-numbing peppercorns. This is great served with rice, which soaks up the sauce.

PREP TIME:
10 minutes

COOK TIME:
20 minutes

2 tablespoons black vinegar

2 tablespoons Chinese light soy sauce

1 tablespoon dark soy sauce

2 tablespoons Shaoxing wine

1/4 teaspoon ground white pepper

3 tablespoons granulated sugar

1/2 teaspoon sea salt

1 1/2 teaspoons cornstarch

1 tablespoon water

2 tablespoons canola oil, plus more for deep-frying

3 medium yellow potatoes (1lb / 454g), peeled and cut into 1/2-inch cubes

2 tablespoons red Sichuan peppercorns

6 dried red facing heaven chili peppers, cut into 1/2-inch segments

1 (1-inch) piece fresh ginger, peeled and thinly sliced

3 garlic cloves, thinly sliced

1 scallion, halved lengthwise and cut crosswise into 1/2-inch lengths

1/3 cup roasted peanuts

1. In a small bowl, mix the black vinegar, light soy sauce, dark soy sauce, rice wine, white pepper, sugar, salt, cornstarch, and water. Set aside.

2. In a deep pot, heat 3 inches of oil over medium-high heat. When a wooden chopstick lowered into the oil immediately sizzles (about 350°F), fry the potatoes for 4 to 5 minutes, until they float. Transfer to a plate with a spider strainer or slotted spoon.

3. In a wok or skillet, heat 2 tablespoons of oil over medium-low heat. Fry the Sichuan peppercorns for 3 to 4 minutes, until they turn dark brown. Remove and discard the peppercorns. Add the chilies to the pan and stir until they darken slightly. Add the ginger, garlic, and scallion to the pan and stir them until fragrant. Add the potatoes and stir for 1 minute over medium-high heat. Add the sauce and stir for about 40 seconds, or until it thickens. Add the peanuts and stir to mix.

PER SERVING: Calories: 371; Total fat: 20g; Saturated fat: 2g; Carbohydrates: 42g; Sugar: 12g; Protein: 6g; Calcium: 46mg

蒜蓉白菜苗 EASY BOK CHOY IN GARLIC SAUCE

This is a popular vegetable dish on Chinese restaurant menus in North America, and it is great as an accompaniment to pretty much any meal. It's healthy and delicious, and it's also easy to make at home. You can use baby bok choy or baby Shanghai bok choy in this dish. Larger bok choy works, too, but I recommend cutting it into halves or quarters lengthwise, or into even smaller pieces, if you are using really big ones.

PREP TIME:
5 minutes

COOK TIME:
5 minutes

16 (4-inch) baby bok choy (16oz / 400g)

1 tablespoon cornstarch

2/3 cup water

2 tablespoons canola oil

4 garlic cloves, minced

1/2 teaspoon sea salt

1/2 teaspoon granulated sugar

1. Trim the root ends from the baby bok choy.

2. In a bowl, mix the cornstarch and water to make a thickener. Set it aside.

3. In a wok or large skillet, heat the oil over high heat until hot. Add the garlic and stir until fragrant. Add the bok choy and cook, stirring constantly, for 2 minutes.

4. Season the bok choy with the salt and sugar. Add the thickener to the pan and continue to stir for 3 minutes to thicken the sauce. Serve hot.

VARIATION: This approach—cooking vegetables with just a bit of garlic and some thickener—works well with a variety of green vegetables such as pea shoots, snow pea leaves, spinach, and broccoli. Just adjust the cooking time for different vegetables.

PER SERVING: Calories: 88; Total fat: 7g; Saturated fat: 0.5g; Carbohydrates: 6g; Sugar: 2g; Protein: 1g; Calcium: 100mg

松仁玉米 PINE NUTS AND SWEET CORN

Song ren yu mi is a classic dish in northeastern Chinese cuisine and Huaiyang cuisine and is popular around the country. Creamy sweet corn, crunchy fragrant pine nuts, and colorful vegetables make this an appealing and memorable dish. This is something that the whole family, including little children, will enjoy.

PREP TIME:
5 minutes

COOK TIME:
5 minutes

2 teaspoons cornstarch

1/2 cup water

1 tablespoon canola oil

1 medium carrot, diced

2 cups frozen corn kernels

1/4 cup frozen peas

1/2 teaspoon sea salt

1 teaspoon granulated sugar

1/3 cup toasted pine nuts

1. In a small bowl, mix the cornstarch and the water to make a thickener. Set it aside.

2. In a wok or skillet, heat the oil over medium-high heat until hot. Add the carrot and stir for 1 minute. Add the corn and peas, season them with the salt and sugar, and stir for 3 minutes.

3. Add the cornstarch mixture and stir everything for 40 seconds to thicken the sauce. Stir in the pine nuts, then immediately remove the pan from the heat. Serve hot.

PREP TIP: If you are starting with untoasted pine nuts, toast them first in a dry skillet over medium heat. Stir constantly to prevent burning for about 3 minutes, or until the pine nuts are golden and fragrant.

PER SERVING: Calories: 188; Total fat: 12g; Saturated fat: 1g; Carbohydrates: 20g; Sugar: 4g; Protein: 4g; Calcium: 12mg

素苍蝇头 BLACK BEAN DRIED TOFU AND GARLIC SCAPES

This is a vegan version of the popular Taiwanese dish called "fly head." Originally a meat dish featuring fermented black beans, it takes its name from the fact that the black beans resemble the heads of flies (though they're infinitely more delicious). This dish has been adapted into a few different vegan versions. Mine uses tofu and fragrant garlic scapes, which have a similar flavor to the Asian chives in the original recipe. I recommend serving this dish with Soy Pulp Cornmeal Buns (page 99), but the bold flavor also goes perfectly with rice.

PREP TIME:
5 minutes

COOK TIME:
5 minutes

1 (8$\frac{1}{2}$ oz / 240g) package five-spiced dried (pressed) tofu

3 tablespoons canola oil

1 teaspoon minced fresh ginger

4 fresh bird's eye chilies, cut into thin rings

2$\frac{1}{2}$ cups (12oz / 350g) $\frac{1}{4}$-inch segments garlic scapes

$\frac{1}{4}$ cup fermented black beans

2 tablespoons Shaoxing wine

2 tablespoons Chinese light soy sauce

2 teaspoons granulated sugar

3 tablespoons water

$\frac{1}{2}$ teaspoon sea salt

$\frac{1}{2}$ teaspoon ground white pepper

1. Cut the dried tofu into $\frac{1}{4}$-inch cubes.

2. In a wok or large skillet, heat the oil over medium heat. Add the ginger and chili and stir until fragrant.

3. Add the dried tofu, garlic scapes, and fermented black beans. Increase the heat to high and stir for 1 minute.

4. Add the wine, soy sauce, sugar, water, salt, and white pepper and cook, stirring constantly, for another 3 minutes. Remove from the heat and serve hot.

VARIATION: Try asparagus, green beans, or Asian chives instead of garlic scapes in this recipe. If using green beans, blanch them first. For those who don't like spicy food, substitute $\frac{1}{4}$ red bell pepper (diced) for the chili peppers.

PER SERVING: Calories: 186; Total fat: 12g; Saturated fat: 1.5g; Carbohydrates: 7g; Sugar: 3g; Protein: 10g; Calcium: 172mg

蚝油芥蓝 CHINESE BROCCOLI IN OYSTER SAUCE

Chinese broccoli in oyster sauce is a classic preparation. Perfectly cooked Chinese broccoli stalks are vibrant and tasty, and the savory-sweet oyster sauce and crunchy garlic chips elevate the flavor of this dish. You will be eating this by the plateful before you know it. It's the perfect vegetable side for any meal.

PREP TIME:
5 minutes

COOK TIME:
10 minutes

1 teaspoon sea salt

2 tablespoons canola oil, divided

1 pound (454g) baby Chinese broccoli

3 tablespoons vegetarian oyster sauce

3 tablespoons water

1 teaspoon Chinese light soy sauce

1 teaspoon granulated sugar

1/4 teaspoon sesame oil

1/8 teaspoon ground white pepper

3 garlic cloves, roughly chopped

1. Bring a large pot of water to a boil over high heat. Add the salt, 1 tablespoon of the canola oil, and the Chinese broccoli. Cook the broccoli for 2 minutes, then immediately drain it in a large colander.

2. In a small bowl, mix the oyster sauce, water, soy sauce, sugar, sesame oil, and white pepper. Set the mixture aside.

3. In a wok or skillet, heat the remaining 1 tablespoon of canola oil over medium heat until hot. Add the garlic and stir for about 1 minute, or until it is golden and crispy. Transfer the garlic immediately to a small bowl, leaving the oil in the pan.

4. Add the sauce mixture to the pan and cook, stirring constantly, for 1 minute to thicken the sauce. Remove it from the heat.

5. Arrange the stalks, all in the same direction, on a plate and pour the sauce over them. Sprinkle the garlic on top.

INGREDIENT TIP: If you can't get baby Chinese broccoli, use mature ones. Split the thick stalks in half lengthwise to ensure that they cook through.

PER SERVING: Calories: 129; Total fat: 8g; Saturated fat: 0.5g; Carbohydrates: 12g; Sugar: 7.5g; Protein: 1g; Calcium: 125mg

醋溜白菜 NAPA CABBAGE STIR-FRY WITH VINEGAR SAUCE

Everyone loves this famous napa cabbage stir-fry (cu liu bai cai) from Shandong cuisine. Shandong is my grandpa's home province. When I was growing up, this was my grandpa's specialty dish at home. The tangy vinegar sauce makes the mild napa cabbage extremely appetizing. While the tender leaves of napa are often more desirable in salads and soups, you can use the crunchy ribs in this delicious stir-fry. I used ribs only here to showcase a dish that utilizes the less-desirable parts of the napa cabbage, but you can use the whole cabbage if you'd prefer (see Tip).

PREP TIME:
10 minutes

COOK TIME:
5 minutes

1 pound 5 ounces (595g) napa cabbage ribs (see Tip)

¼ cup white rice vinegar

¼ cup Chinese light soy sauce

2 tablespoons water

1 tablespoon cornstarch

1 teaspoon granulated sugar

2 tablespoons canola oil

4 dried red facing heaven chili peppers, cut into ½-inch segments

4 garlic cloves, minced

1. Split the large cabbage ribs in half lengthwise. Holding the knife at a 30-degree angle to the cutting board, angle-cut the ribs into ¼- to ½-inch-thick slices. You should end up with about 8½ cups lightly packed.

2. In a small bowl, mix the rice vinegar, soy sauce, water, cornstarch, and sugar. Set the sauce mixture aside.

3. In a large wok or skillet, heat the oil over high heat until hot. Add the chili and garlic and stir until fragrant. Add the cabbage and stir for 3 minutes, or until the cabbage softens.

4. Pour in the sauce mixture and stir the cabbage for 1 minute to thicken the sauce. Serve hot.

INGREDIENT TIP: To separate the tender leaves from the sturdy ribs, you can cut the head of cabbage crosswise where the ribs more or less end. Alternatively, you can tear the leafy portions off the ribs one leaf at a time. You can also use the whole cabbage leaves, including the ribs. If you do, stir-fry the ribs first for 2 minutes and then add the leaves to stir-fry for 1 minute before adding the sauce.

PER SERVING: Calories: 114; Total fat: 7.5g; Saturated fat: 0.5g; Carbohydrates: 10g; Sugar: 3.5g; Protein: 3g; Calcium: 184mg

干煸菜花 DRY-FRIED CAULIFLOWER

Dry-fried cauliflower is an extremely popular dish in China, both at home and in restaurants. The dish is typically made with pork belly, but you will be surprised by how good it is without the meat. This is a quick and easy dish yet extremely flavorful. This dry-frying technique is often used to cook cauliflower and green beans, but it can be used for a variety of other vegetables, such as potatoes and lotus roots.

PREP TIME:
10 minutes

COOK TIME:
5 minutes

1 medium head cauliflower
(1lb 5oz / 595g)

1 scallion

1 tablespoon canola oil, plus
more for deep-frying

3 garlic cloves, sliced

2 fresh bird's eye chilies,
sliced into thin rings

2 tablespoons Chinese light
soy sauce

3/4 teaspoon sea salt

3/4 teaspoon granulated sugar

1. Cut the cauliflower florets into bite-size pieces and then cut the stems into pieces of about the same size. Halve the scallion lengthwise, then cut it crosswise into 1-inch segments.

2. In a large deep pot, heat at least 3 inches of oil over high heat. When the oil is very hot and begins to smoke (425°F), lower the cauliflower into the oil all in one batch and deep-fry for 30 seconds, or until it is lightly golden. Using a spider strainer or slotted spoon, remove the cauliflower.

3. In a wok or large skillet, heat 1 tablespoon of oil over high heat. Add the scallion, garlic, and chilies and stir until fragrant.

4. Add the cauliflower to the wok and stir for 1 minute. Add the soy sauce, salt, and sugar and stir for another minute to thoroughly combine everything. Remove the pan from the heat. Serve hot.

VARIATION: To try this dish with green beans, deep-fry the beans for about 1½ minutes to thoroughly cook them before stir-frying.

PER SERVING: Calories: 122; Total fat: 10g; Saturated fat: 1g; Carbohydrates: 5g; Sugar: 2g; Protein: 1g; Calcium: 30mg

地三鲜 SAUTÉED POTATO, GREEN PEPPERS, AND EGGPLANT

This mix of vegetables flavored with a rich sauce is a classic savory dish from northeastern Chinese cuisine. Its name, di san xian, literally translates as "three delicious seasonal vegetables grown in the soil."

PREP TIME:
10 minutes

COOK TIME:
5 minutes

1 large yellow potato (8oz / 225g), peeled

1 teaspoon cornstarch, plus 2 tablespoons, divided

1 large Chinese eggplant, or 1/2 globe eggplant

1 teaspoon distilled white vinegar

2 teaspoons canola oil, plus more for deep-frying

1 green bell pepper, cut into bite-size pieces

3/4 cup water

2 teaspoons dark soy sauce

1 tablespoon Shaoxing wine

1 tablespoon vegetarian oyster sauce

2 teaspoons granulated sugar

3/4 teaspoon sea salt

4 garlic cloves, minced

1 scallion, thinly sliced

1. Split the potato lengthwise into quarters, then roll-cut the quarters (see page 6). Bring a pot of water to a boil. Cook the potato for 5 minutes, until you can pierce them with a chopstick. Drain and toss with 1 teaspoon of cornstarch.

2. Roll-cut the eggplant into pieces the same size as the potato. Transfer the eggplant to a bowl and toss with the vinegar and 1 tablespoon of cornstarch. In a small bowl, mix the water, soy sauce, wine, oyster sauce, sugar, salt, and the remaining 1 tablespoon of cornstarch.

3. In a deep pot, heat at least 3 inches of oil over medium-high heat. When a wooden chopstick lowered into the oil immediately sizzles (350ºF), fry the eggplant for 1½ minutes, then use a spider strainer to remove and set it aside. Fry the potato for 1½ minutes and remove. Fry the bell pepper for 30 seconds, then remove.

4. In a wok or skillet, heat 2 teaspoons of oil over high heat. Add the garlic and scallion and stir until fragrant. Add the sauce and stir for 1 minute to thicken. Add the vegetables and stir for 30 seconds to coat with the sauce. Serve hot.

PER SERVING: Calories: 220; Total fat: 10g; Saturated fat: 1g; Carbohydrates: 29g; Sugar: 7.5g; Protein: 2g; Calcium: 23mg

韭菜炒豆芽 STIR-FRIED BEAN SPROUTS WITH ASIAN CHIVES

This is a quick and easy homestyle dish. Bean sprouts are nutritious and commonly used in Chinese cuisine. Asian chives (also sold as garlic chives) may not be very easy to come by, but they are totally worth hunting down for their flavor. This dish is seasoned simply, with just some salt, so that you can taste the natural sweetness of the fresh bean sprouts and chives. This dish is often paired with Spring Pancakes (page 92) but works well as a side dish for pretty much any kind of meal.

PREP TIME:
5 minutes

COOK TIME:
5 minutes

1 tablespoon canola oil

1 tablespoon sliced scallions

1 teaspoon minced
fresh ginger

6 cups (1lb / 454g) lightly
packed bean sprouts

2 cups (3½ oz / 100g) 2-inch
lengths Asian chives

1¼ teaspoons sea salt

1. In a wok or skillet, heat the oil over high heat until hot. Add the scallions and ginger and stir until fragrant.

2. Add the bean sprouts and stir for 1 minute, or until soft. Add the chive, season with the salt, and stir for 2 minutes. Serve hot.

PREP TIP: After washing the bean sprouts, make sure to completely drain them to avoid soggy bean sprouts in the stir-fry.

INGREDIENT TIP: The bean sprouts in this dish are typically mung bean sprouts, and I prefer them because they are more tender. But you can use soybean sprouts as well if that's what's available in your market. Soybean sprouts are thicker with a bigger head, and they require a slightly longer cooking time.

PER SERVING: Calories: 75; Total fat: 3.5g; Saturated fat: 0.5g; Carbohydrates: 8g; Sugar: 4.5g; Protein: 3g; Calcium: 34mg

虎皮尖椒 TIGER SKIN LONG HOT PEPPERS

This dish, hu pi jian jiao—which means "tiger skin long hot pepper"—is so named because the green long hot peppers are cooked until their outsides are blistered and blackened. Some restaurant chefs deep-fry the peppers, but at home you can char them in a wok to create the same look (and a healthier dish). Spicy food lovers will enjoy this dish!

PREP TIME:
5 minutes

COOK TIME:
10 minutes

1 tablespoon black vinegar

1 tablespoon water

1 teaspoon dark soy sauce

1 teaspoon granulated sugar

1/2 teaspoon sea salt

1 pound (454g) green long hot peppers

2 tablespoons canola oil

6 garlic cloves, roughly chopped

2 tablespoons fermented black beans

1. In a small bowl, mix the black vinegar, water, soy sauce, sugar, and salt. Set the sauce aside.

2. Remove the stems from the peppers, cut a long slit down the length of each pepper, and use the slit to remove the seeds. Cut the peppers in half crosswise.

3. Heat a wok over medium-high heat. Add the peppers and press on them with a ladle to char their skins, turning the peppers to char both sides, for about 10 minutes, or until all the peppers are blackened, blistered, and limp. Transfer the peppers to a plate.

4. Reduce the heat to medium-low and add the oil, garlic, and black beans to the wok. Stir until fragrant. Return the peppers to the wok and increase the heat to high. Add the sauce and stir the peppers for about 30 seconds so they take on the flavor. Serve hot.

INGREDIENT TIP: These peppers are sometimes labeled Italian long hots, but in Chinese supermarkets they usually go by long hot peppers. If you can't find them, use green bell peppers or shishito peppers instead and add a few bird's eye chilies for the spicy kick: Cut the bird's eye chilies into small rings and stir-fry them with the garlic and black beans before adding the bell or shishito peppers.

PER SERVING: Calories: 119; Total fat: 7.5g; Saturated fat: 0.5g; Carbohydrates: 1g; Sugar: 4.5g; Protein: 5g; Calcium: 18mg

西芹百合炒腰果 STIR-FRIED CELERY, LILY BULBS, AND CASHEWS

This recipe combines delicate lily bulbs, aromatic celery, and nutty cashews in a fragrant dish full of interesting textures. This light stir-fry looks very elegant when it's plated, and it works well as a side to balance out any main dish with a strong flavor.

PREP TIME:
5 minutes, plus
4 to 6 hours to rehydrate

COOK TIME:
5 minutes

½ cup (1½ oz / 40g) dried lily bulbs, soaked in cool water for 4 to 6 hours

5 large celery stalks, leaves trimmed off

4 teaspoons canola oil, divided

1 teaspoon sea salt, divided

2 teaspoons cornstarch

½ cup water

1 teaspoon granulated sugar

½ cup unsalted roasted cashews

1. Using a paring knife, scrape any blemishes and dark spots from the lily bulbs. Remove tough strings from the celery and split the larger stalks in half lengthwise. Cut the celery at an angle into thick diamond-shaped slices.

2. Bring a medium pot of water to a boil over high heat. Add 2 teaspoons of oil, ½ teaspoon of salt, and the celery and cook for 1½ minutes, to partially cook the celery. Add the lily bulbs to the pot and cook for 30 seconds. Drain the celery and lily bulbs in a colander.

3. In a small bowl, mix the cornstarch and water to make a thickener. Set it aside.

4. In a wok or skillet, heat the remaining 2 teaspoons of oil over medium-high heat until hot. Add the celery, lily bulbs, sugar, and the remaining ½ teaspoon of salt and stir for 1 minute. Add the cornstarch mixture and stir for 30 seconds to thicken the sauce. Remove the pan from the heat, sprinkle in the cashews, and mix everything together. Serve hot.

PREP TIP: Blanching the celery and lily bulbs with salt and oil give them a softer texture and a more vibrant color. If you prefer crunchy celery, reduce the blanching time.

PER SERVING: Calories: 185; Total fat: 13g; Saturated fat: 2g; Carbohydrates: 16g; Sugar: 3g; Protein: 3g; Calcium: 38mg

Mapo Tofu,
PAGE 52

4

Soups, Stews, and Braises

麻婆豆腐 MAPO TOFU

This is my favorite tofu dish. Tender tofu stewed in a spicy, savory sauce, it represents the best flavors of Sichuan cuisine. The traditional dish uses ground meat, but my version is vegan. The spiciness comes from doubanjiang (fermented chili bean paste), dried chili, and Sichuan peppercorn powder.

PREP TIME:
10 minutes

COOK TIME:
10 minutes

1/4 cup canola oil

1 1/4 cups (3 1/2 oz / 100g) 1/4-inch diced king oyster mushrooms

3 tablespoons doubanjiang

1 tablespoon finely chopped fermented black beans

4 garlic cloves, minced

1 tablespoon minced fresh ginger

1 scallion, thinly sliced, divided

1 teaspoon chili pepper powder

3 teaspoons red Sichuan peppercorn powder, divided

1 3/4 cups water, divided

1 tablespoon Shaoxing wine

1 tablespoon Chinese light soy sauce

1/2 teaspoon granulated sugar

1 (16oz / 454g) block store-bought tofu (see Tip) or 2/3 recipe Tofu from Scratch (page 107), cut into 3/4-inch cubes

1 tablespoon cornstarch

1. In a wok or skillet, heat the oil over medium-high heat until hot. Add the mushroom and stir-fry for 4 minutes, or until lightly browned.

2. Add the doubanjiang, black beans, garlic, ginger, and half of the scallion and stir for 1 minute, or until fragrant. Add the chili powder and 2 teaspoons of Sichuan peppercorn powder and stir for 30 seconds. Add 1½ cups water and the wine, soy sauce, and sugar and bring to a boil. Add the tofu and cook for 5 minutes.

3. In a small bowl, mix the remaining 1/4 cup of water and cornstarch and add it to the wok. Cook for 1 to 2 minutes, until the sauce is reduced and thickened.

4. Transfer everything to a deep dish. Sprinkle the remaining 1 teaspoon of Sichuan peppercorn powder and the other half of the scallion on top and serve hot.

PER SERVING: Calories: 261; Total fat: 18g; Saturated fat: 1g; Carbohydrates: 11g; Sugar: 1g; Protein: 16g; Calcium: 220mg

红烧面筋 RED-BRAISED GLUTEN BALLS

Red-braised gluten balls are commonly stuffed with a pork filling, but they are just as delicious without the meat. Simmered slowly, the porous gluten balls soak up the tasty broth and become tender, making them a satisfying main dish.

PREP TIME:
5 minutes, plus 2 hours or up to overnight to rehydrate

COOK TIME:
15 minutes

8 medium dried shiitake mushrooms (³/₄ oz / 20g), soaked in cool water for 2 hours or up to overnight

4 to 5 cups (6oz / 180g) Fried Gluten Balls (page 105) or store-bought fried gluten balls, thawed if frozen

2 tablespoons canola oil

1 tablespoon minced fresh ginger

2 fresh bird's eye chilies, cut into thin rings

1 whole star anise

3 tablespoons Chinese light soy sauce

1 teaspoon dark soy sauce

2 teaspoons granulated sugar

2 tablespoons Shaoxing wine

1 cup water, divided

1 teaspoon cornstarch

1 tablespoon finely chopped fresh cilantro

1. Drain the mushrooms, reserving 1 cup of the soaking water. Discard the tough mushroom stems and thinly slice the caps. Use the tip of a knife to cut a small hole into each gluten ball (so they will absorb the broth).

2. In a wok, heat the oil over medium heat until hot. Add the ginger, chili, star anise, and mushroom and stir for about 1 minute, or until fragrant.

3. Add the gluten balls, light soy sauce, dark soy sauce, sugar, wine, ½ cup of water, and the reserved mushroom soaking water. Increase the heat to high and bring the mixture to a boil. Reduce the heat to medium-low, cover the wok with a lid, and simmer everything for 10 minutes.

4. In a small bowl, mix the cornstarch and the remaining ½ cup of water together, then add the mixture to the wok. Increase the heat to medium-high and stir for 1 minute to thicken the sauce. Remove the wok from the heat and serve hot, garnished with the cilantro.

PER SERVING: Calories: 247; Total fat: 18g; Saturated fat: 1.5g; Carbohydrates: 11g; Sugar: 3g; Protein: 7g; Calcium: 33mg

罗汉斋 BUDDHA'S DELIGHT

This Cantonese New Year's dish traditionally boasts 18 vegan delicacies, often including lily flowers, mushrooms, bamboo shoots, and glass noodles. The recipe is flexible, and families often use different combinations of ingredients.

PREP TIME:
20 minutes, plus 2 hours or up to overnight to rehydrate

COOK TIME:
20 minutes

6 medium dried shiitake mushrooms (1/2 oz / 15g), soaked in cool water for 2 hours or up to overnight

1/4 cup (1/4 oz / 7g) dried wood ear mushrooms, soaked in cool water for 2 to 4 hours

1/4 cup (1/3 oz / 10g) dried lily flowers, soaked in warm water for 30 minutes

1 (1 1/2 oz / 40g) bunch glass noodles, soaked in cool water for 15 minutes

8 sugar snap peas or snow peas

3 tablespoons Chinese light soy sauce

3 tablespoons vegetarian oyster sauce

1 tablespoon cornstarch

2 tablespoons canola oil

5 Tofu Puffs (page 108) or store-bought tofu puffs, halved

2 cups water

1/2 medium carrot, thinly sliced

1/2 cup canned straw mushrooms

3 cups (5oz / 150g) roughly chopped napa cabbage

8 fresh or canned baby corn

1 cup roughly chopped Chinese mustard greens (1 3/4 oz / 50g)

1/4 cup thinly sliced canned bamboo shoots

1 tablespoon sesame oil

1. Drain the soaked ingredients, reserving 1 cup of the shiitake soaking water. Discard the tough stems from the shiitake, tough roots from the wood ear mushrooms, and tough ends of the lily flowers. String the peas. Halve or quarter the shiitake caps (depending on their size).

2. In a small bowl, mix the shiitake soaking water, soy sauce, oyster sauce, and cornstarch. Set the sauce mixture aside.

3. In a soup pot, heat the canola oil over medium heat until hot. Add the shiitake and wood ear mushrooms and stir for 1 minute. Add the lily flowers and tofu puffs and stir for 1 minute. Add the water, increase the heat to high, and bring everything to a boil. Cover the pot, reduce the heat to medium, and simmer the mixture for 5 minutes.

4. Stir in the carrot and straw mushrooms, then pour in the sauce mixture. Increase the heat to high and bring everything to a boil. Add the napa cabbage, baby corn, and glass noodles, lower the heat to medium, and simmer the vegetables for 5 minutes.

5. Add the mustard green, bamboo shoots, and peas and simmer them for 3 minutes.

6. Remove the pot from the heat. Serve hot drizzled with sesame oil.

PER SERVING: Calories: 195; Total fat: 11g; Saturated fat: 1g; Carbohydrates: 19g; Sugar: 5.5g; Protein: 6g; Calcium: 90mg

西兰花烩双菇 BROCCOLI WITH BRAISED MUSHROOMS

This is a very popular vegetable side dish on restaurant menus because it's healthy and full of rich umami flavor. The velvety sauce from the mushrooms coats the blanched broccoli, making it wonderfully delicious.

PREP TIME:
10 minutes, plus 2 hours or up to overnight to rehydrate

COOK TIME:
15 minutes

4 medium dried shiitake mushrooms (¹/₃ oz / 10g), soaked in cool water for 2 hours or up to overnight

1 tablespoon Chinese light soy sauce

1 tablespoon vegetarian oyster sauce

¹/₂ teaspoon ground white pepper

1 teaspoon cornstarch

¹/₃ cup water

1 tablespoon sea salt, plus ¹/₄ teaspoon

4 tablespoons canola oil, divided

5 cups (9oz / 250g) bite-size broccoli florets

2 teaspoons minced fresh ginger

3 cups (7oz / 200g) ¹/₄-inch-thick slices king oyster mushrooms

1. Drain the mushrooms, reserving ⅓ cup of the soaking water. Discard the tough stems and cut the caps into halves or quarters (depending on their size).

2. In a small bowl, mix the soy sauce, oyster sauce, white pepper, and mushroom soaking water to make a sauce. In another small bowl, mix the cornstarch and water to make a thickener. Set both aside.

3. Bring a large pot of water to a boil over high heat. Add 1 tablespoon of salt, 1 tablespoon of oil, and the broccoli. Blanch the broccoli for 2½ to 3 minutes, until it's cooked. Remove it immediately using a spider strainer or slotted spoon.

4. In a wok or skillet, heat the remaining 3 tablespoons of oil over medium heat until hot. Add the ginger and stir until fragrant. Add the shiitake and king oyster mushrooms and remaining ¼ teaspoon of salt. Stir-fry the mushrooms over medium-high heat for 5 minutes, or until they shrink a bit.

5. Reduce the heat to medium-low and add the sauce. Cover the pan and simmer the mushrooms for 3 minutes.

6. Add the cornstarch mixture, increase the heat to medium-high, and stir the mushrooms until the sauce thickens.

7. To serve, arrange the broccoli on a plate in a circle with the florets facing outward. Pour the mushrooms into the middle.

PER SERVING: Calories: 151; Total fat: 12g; Saturated fat: 1g; Carbohydrates: 9g; Sugar: 4g; Protein: 3g; Calcium: 38mg

红烧茄子 RED-BRAISED EGGPLANTS

This is a classic dish enjoyed across China in both homes and restaurants. The tender eggplants are cooked to perfection and glazed in a spicy, sweet, and savory sauce. This sauce also gives the dish a dark reddish-brown color, a cooking technique famously known as red-braising or red-cooking.

PREP TIME:
20 minutes

COOK TIME:
5 minutes

3 medium Chinese eggplants (1lb 5oz / 595g)

2 teaspoons sea salt

2 tablespoons Chinese light soy sauce

1 teaspoon dark soy sauce

4 teaspoons granulated sugar

2 tablespoons Shaoxing wine

3/4 cup water

1 tablespoon cornstarch

1/4 cup canola oil

6 garlic cloves, minced

2 fresh bird's eye chilies, cut into thin rings

1 tablespoon sliced scallion

1. Roll-cut the eggplants (see page 6) into 3-inch-long pieces about 1 inch thick. In a large bowl, toss the eggplant pieces with the salt and let them rest for 10 minutes.

2. Meanwhile, in a small bowl, mix the light soy sauce, dark soy sauce, sugar, wine, and ¼ cup of water to make a sauce. In another small bowl, mix the cornstarch and ½ cup of water together to make a thickener.

3. Squeeze the salted eggplant to release as much moisture as possible. Set the eggplant aside.

4. In a wok or large skillet, heat the oil over high heat until the oil begins to smoke. Add the eggplant and stir for 1 minute. Add the garlic and chili and stir for 1 minute. Add the sauce and continue stirring for another 2 minutes. Add the cornstarch mixture and stir for 1 minute to thicken the sauce.

5. Remove the pan from the heat. Serve hot garnished with the scallion.

PER SERVING: Calories: 196; Total fat: 14g; Saturated fat: 1g; Carbohydrates: 13g; Sugar: 7g; Protein: 2g; Calcium: 21mg

四季豆烧土豆 BRAISED GREEN BEANS AND POTATOES

This dish of fried potatoes and green beans simmered in a savory sauce is a classic homestyle dish that is both tasty and comforting. Keeping the pieces of potato small will allow them to really absorb the flavor of the sauce as they braise alongside the green beans. This dish comes together quickly for weeknight meals and can be served as a side or with rice for a substantial meal.

PREP TIME:
15 minutes

COOK TIME:
5 minutes

2 medium yellow potatoes (10½ oz / 300g)

3 tablespoons canola oil

2 cups halved and trimmed green beans

4 garlic cloves, minced

1 tablespoon Chinese light soy sauce

1 tablespoon vegetarian oyster sauce

½ teaspoon sea salt

½ teaspoon granulated sugar

¾ cup water

1. Peel the potatoes and quarter them lengthwise. Roll-cut them (see page 6) into small, bite-size pieces no thicker than ½ inch and 1½ inches long.

2. In a wok or a large skillet, heat the oil over medium-high heat until it just begins to smoke. Add the green beans and stir for 1 minute. Add the potato and stir for 2 minutes. Add the garlic and stir for 1 minute.

3. Add the soy sauce, oyster sauce, salt, sugar, and water. Simmer the potato and green beans uncovered, stirring constantly to make sure all the pieces cook evenly, for about 8 minutes, or until the liquid is reduced and just coating the vegetables.

4. Serve hot.

PER SERVING: Calories: 195; Total fat: 10g; Saturated fat: 1g; Carbohydrates: 24g; Sugar: 5g; Protein: 3g; Calcium: 45mg

番茄菜花 TOMATO-BRAISED CAULIFLOWER

This is an easy homestyle dish and one of my personal favorite vegetable preparations. Tender cauliflower bites smothered in tangy and savory tomato sauce make for a great side dish to be enjoyed by the whole family. Serve this with a side of rice; children will love the rice soaked in the tomato sauce.

PREP TIME:
5 minutes

COOK TIME:
15 minutes

1/2 large head cauliflower (1lb 3oz / 540g)

2 tablespoons canola oil

2 garlic cloves, minced

2 medium tomatoes, cut into 1-inch chunks

1/3 cup water

1 1/4 teaspoons sea salt

1/4 teaspoon granulated sugar

1. Cut the cauliflower florets into even bite-size pieces. Cut the stem into the same size pieces.

2. In a skillet, heat the oil over medium heat until hot. Add the garlic and stir until fragrant. Add the tomato, increase the heat to medium-high, and stir-fry for another 3 minutes, or until the tomato chunks have fallen apart.

3. Add the water, salt, sugar, and cauliflower and stir to combine. When the tomato sauce starts to bubble, cover the skillet with a lid. Reduce the heat to medium-low and simmer the cauliflower for 7 minutes, or until just tender.

4. Serve hot.

PREP TIP: Some cooks will blanch the tomatoes in boiling water and peel off the skin before using them in this recipe. I use this quicker method, but feel free to add this additional step if you wish to produce a tomato sauce without pieces of tomato skin, for better presentation and mouthfeel.

PER SERVING: Calories: 115; Total fat: 7.5g; Saturated fat: 0.5g; Carbohydrates: 11g; Sugar: 5g; Protein: 4g; Calcium: 42mg

蒜蓉平菇 BRAISED OYSTER MUSHROOMS IN GARLIC SAUCE

Oyster mushrooms are a tasty delicacy that don't require a strong-flavored sauce. Keeping the ingredients simple in this beloved family favorite allows the oyster mushrooms to shine. This is a tasty side for any main dish; I also love these saucy oyster mushrooms on their own over rice.

PREP TIME:
5 minutes

COOK TIME:
15 minutes

3 tablespoons canola oil

4 garlic cloves, minced

3 tablespoons sliced scallions

12 cups (1lb 5oz / 600g) bite-size pieces oyster mushrooms

2 cups water, divided

1¹/₂ teaspoons sea salt

4 teaspoons cornstarch

2 tablespoons chopped fresh cilantro

1. In a wok or skillet, heat the oil over medium heat until hot. Add the garlic and scallions and stir until fragrant.

2. Add the mushrooms, increase the heat to high, and stir for 3 minutes, or until the mushrooms shrink by half.

3. Add 1 cup of water and the salt. When everything comes to a boil, reduce the heat to medium-low, cover the pan with a lid, and simmer the mushrooms for 5 minutes.

4. Meanwhile, in a small bowl, mix the cornstarch with 1 cup of water to make a thickener.

5. Add the cornstarch mixture to the wok, increase the heat to high, and stir the mushrooms for another 2 to 3 minutes, until the sauce comes to a full boil.

6. Sprinkle the cilantro into the wok and stir to mix before removing it from the heat.

PER SERVING: Calories: 159; Total fat: 11g; Saturated fat: 1g; Carbohydrates: 13g; Sugar: 2g; Protein: 5g; Calcium: 14mg

素酸辣汤 VEGAN HOT AND SOUR SOUP

This famous dish, which originated in Sichuan, is a perfect, warming soup for winter and is loved around the country. The hot and sour taste comes from ground white pepper and black vinegar. The ingredients used in the soup vary in different regions of China but often include eggs, tofu, meat, wood ear mushrooms, and various vegetables. Here is my take on a vegan version of the dish.

PREP TIME:
10 minutes, plus
2 to 4 hours to rehydrate

COOK TIME:
10 minutes

1/4 cup (1/4 oz / 7g) dried wood ear mushrooms, soaked in cool water for 2 to 4 hours

1/4 cup (1/3 oz / 10g) dried lily flowers, soaked in warm water for 30 minutes

2 1/2 cups (5oz / 150g) enoki mushrooms

6 cups water

7 ounces (200g) store-bought firm tofu or Tofu from Scratch (page 107), cut into 2-inch-long, 1/4-inch-thick strips

1 teaspoon sea salt

5 tablespoons black vinegar

3 tablespoons Chinese light soy sauce

4 teaspoons ground white pepper

1/4 cup cornstarch

2 teaspoons sesame oil

1/4 cup chopped fresh cilantro

1 scallion, thinly sliced

1. Remove the tough root ends from the wood ear mushrooms and the tough ends of the lily flowers, and trim the roots off the enoki mushrooms.

2. Cut the wood ear mushrooms into thin strips, tear the lily flowers in half lengthwise, and pull the enoki mushrooms apart.

3. In a large pot, bring the water to a boil over high heat. Add both mushrooms, the tofu, lily flowers, and the salt and bring everything to a boil. Reduce the heat to medium and simmer for 8 minutes.

4. Meanwhile, in a small bowl, mix the vinegar, soy sauce, white pepper, and cornstarch, stirring to dissolve the pepper and cornstarch.

5. Pour the vinegar mixture into the pot, increase the heat to high, and stir for 1 minute, or until the liquid comes to a full boil again and thickens. Remove the pot from the heat and stir in the sesame oil.

6. Serve hot, garnished with the cilantro and scallion.

VARIATION: You can add or swap other ingredients into this soup, such as bamboo shoots, carrots, or rehydrated dried shiitake mushrooms, to add new flavors and textures.

PER SERVING: Calories: 104; Total fat: 2.5g; Saturated fat: 0.5g; Carbohydrates: 14g; Sugar: 1.5g; Protein: 2g; Calcium: 29mg

白菜粉丝面筋汤
NAPA CABBAGE, GLASS NOODLES, AND GLUTEN BALL SOUP

In this cozy soup, sweet napa cabbage, slippery glass noodles, and delicious protein-rich fried gluten are simmered together in a plain broth. This soup is as simple as can be yet so comforting to have as a side dish or a light meal.

PREP TIME:
5 minutes,
plus
15 minutes to
rehydrate

COOK TIME:
20 minutes

6 cups water

6 cups (10¹/₂ oz / 300g) tightly packed roughly chopped napa cabbage

10 Fried Gluten Balls (page 105) or store-bought gluten balls, halved

1 (1¹/₂ oz / 40g) bunch glass noodles, soaked in cool water for 15 minutes

2 teaspoons sea salt

¹/₂ teaspoon ground white pepper

¹/₄ cup chopped fresh cilantro

1. In a large pot, bring the water to a boil over high heat. Add the cabbage, gluten balls, and glass noodles. Season with the salt and white pepper.

2. Bring the water back to a boil. Reduce the heat to medium, cover, and simmer the soup for 8 minutes.

3. Stir in the cilantro before serving. Serve hot.

INGREDIENT TIP: You can use the entire cabbage leaf in this soup, but I like to mostly use the tender portions of the leaves and save the sturdier ribs for a recipe like Napa Cabbage Stir-Fry with Vinegar Sauce (page 44).

VARIATION: Try winter melon instead of napa cabbage in this soup. Napa cabbage is often eaten in the winter, while winter melon is often eaten in the summer.

PER SERVING: Calories: 115; Total fat: 6g; Saturated fat: 0.5g; Carbohydrates: 12g; Sugar: 1g; Protein: 4g; Calcium: 88mg

番茄土豆卷心菜汤 TOMATO, POTATO, AND CABBAGE SOUP

Tomato, potato, and cabbage are a classic combination in Chinese soups. In this delicious version, you can taste the sweetness of the cabbage and potatoes and the tanginess of the tomatoes. A dash of rice wine and a few slices of ginger add depth of flavor and warm the body during cold months. This healthy soup can be served as a side dish or a light meal on its own.

PREP TIME:
10 minutes

COOK TIME:
30 minutes

6 cups water

2 medium tomatoes, cut into 1-inch pieces

2 medium potatoes (10½ oz / 300g), peeled and cut into 1-inch pieces

4 cups (7oz / 200g) bite-size squares Taiwanese flat cabbage or green cabbage

1 (1-inch) piece fresh ginger, thinly sliced

¼ cup Shaoxing wine

2½ teaspoons sea salt

1. In a large pot, bring the water to a boil over high heat. Add the tomato, potato, cabbage, ginger, wine, and salt and return the liquid to a boil.

2. Reduce the heat to medium, cover the pot, and simmer the soup for 15 minutes, until all of the vegetables are tender.

3. Serve hot.

PER SERVING: Calories: 109; Total fat: 0.5g; Saturated fat: 0g; Carbohydrates: 21g; Sugar: 5.5g; Protein: 3g; Calcium: 48mg

紫菜冻豆腐汤 SEA LAVER AND FROZEN TOFU SOUP

Sea laver, an edible seaweed, adds lots of flavor and umami to a plain soup. Purple sea laver (zi cai) usually comes packaged as round sheets. Be careful not to confuse this product with Japanese nori, which is flattened into a paper-thin rectangle for wrapping sushi. Frozen tofu adds a spongy texture to this soup, but if you don't have any on hand, you can use fresh tofu instead.

PREP TIME:
5 minutes

COOK TIME:
20 minutes

2¹⁄₂ cups (5oz / 150g) enoki mushrooms

6 cups water

10¹⁄₂ ounces (300g) frozen firm tofu slices (see Tip)

¹⁄₂ cup (¹⁄₄ oz / 5g) lightly packed small pieces of dried sea laver

1³⁄₄ teaspoons sea salt

2 teaspoons sesame oil

1. Remove the tough roots of the enoki. Tear the mushroom strands apart into individual pieces.

2. In a large pot, bring the water to boil over high heat. Add the tofu, mushrooms, sea laver, and salt and bring the liquid back to a full boil. Reduce the heat to medium and simmer the soup for 5 minutes.

3. Remove the pot from the heat and drizzle in the sesame oil. Serve hot.

INGREDIENT TIP: When you have unused fresh tofu that will expire soon, you can slice it up and keep it in the freezer, which preserves it and also gives it a wonderful spongy texture. I often freeze my tofu just so that I can have spongy tofu to eat. These slices can be added straight into this soup; you'll need to freeze about ²⁄₃ of a standard 16oz tofu block to have the right amount for this recipe. (This method works best with tofu that is medium-firm, firm, or extra-firm.) You can also buy frozen tofu, as it is a very popular ingredient for making Chinese soups and stews.

PER SERVING: Calories: 98; Total fat: 5.5g; Saturated fat: 0.5g; Carbohydrates: 5g; Sugar: 0.5g; Protein: 8g; Calcium: 140mg

南瓜银耳羹 PUMPKIN AND SNOW FUNGUS SOUP

Food therapy is an important part of Chinese cuisine. The nourishing ingredients in this soup strengthen the digestive system, calm the mind, and promote beauty. It is ideal for autumn and winter but can be made all year round. Use rock sugar, if you can, for its medicinal properties; if you don't have rock sugar, use granulated sugar or a healthy sweetener of your choice.

PREP TIME:
10 minutes, plus
3 to 4 hours
to rehydrate

COOK TIME:
2 hours
10 minutes

1/2 head dried snow fungus (1/2 oz / 15g), soaked in cool water for 3 to 4 hours

16 dried lotus seeds

7 cups water

11/2 cups (7oz / 200g) 1-inch cubes sugar pumpkin

1/4 cup jujubes, halved and pitted

2 tablespoons goji berries

1/4 cup rock sugar

1. Using a pair of scissors, remove the tough yellow core of the snow fungus, then cut the outer fronds into small pieces. Place the snow fungus, lotus seeds, and water into a large clay or stainless steel soup pot.

2. Bring the water to a boil over high heat, then reduce the heat to medium-low and simmer, covered, for 1 hour 30 minutes.

3. Add the pumpkin and jujubes and add a little more water, if needed, to cover the ingredients. Bring the soup to a boil over high heat, then reduce the heat to medium-low, and simmer for 15 minutes. Add the goji berries and rock sugar and simmer for a final 10 minutes. Remove the pot from the heat.

4. Serve this soup hot or cold, as dessert, tonic, or snack.

PREP TIP: Making this soup takes patience. You need sufficient soaking time and slow cooking to produce soft and gelatinous snow fungus. Do not rehydrate the dried lotus seeds before cooking them; if you do, they will not soften when boiled.

VARIATION: Try this soup with papaya or Asian pear instead of pumpkin. Papaya promotes beauty and Asian pear nourishes the lungs.

PER SERVING: Calories: 115; Total fat: 0g; Saturated fat: 0g; Carbohydrates: 28g; Sugar: 19g; Protein: 2g; Calcium: 28mg

Eight Treasure Congee,
PAGE 81

5

Rice, Noodles, and Congee

孜然土豆炒饭 CUMIN POTATO FRIED RICE

In my hometown, Beijing, Uighur cuisine from China's western Xinjiang Province is extremely popular. Uighur cooks use a lot of cumin in a variety of dishes to add a kick and smokiness, and this fried rice is inspired by that style of cooking. Potato fried rice is my favorite kind of fried rice, as I love the heartiness of this combination. If you like spicy foods, add a little Sichuan Chili Oil (page 110).

PREP TIME:
5 minutes

COOK TIME:
10 minutes

2 medium potatoes
(10¹/₂ oz / 300g)

3 tablespoons canola oil

¹/₂ large onion, cut into
¹/₄-inch cubes

1 small carrot, peeled and cut
into ¹/₄-inch cubes

4 teaspoons ground cumin

¹/₂ teaspoon five-spice powder

2 tablespoons Chinese light
soy sauce

3 cups cooked rice

³/₄ teaspoon sea salt

1 tablespoon toasted white
sesame seeds

1. Peel the potatoes and cut into ¹/₄-inch cubes. Immediately soak the potato in a bowl of water to wash off the starch, then drain them in a colander.

2. In a wok or nonstick skillet, heat the oil over medium-high heat. Add the onion and carrot and stir for 2 minutes, or until fragrant.

3. Add the potato and stir for 3 minutes. Reduce the heat to medium and add the cumin, five-spice powder, and soy sauce. Stir for another 2 minutes, or until the potato is cooked through.

4. Break up any lumps in the rice and add the rice to the pan. Increase the heat to medium-high, then flip the rice and other ingredients for 1 minute to combine.

5. Season the mixture with the salt, then flip and stir everything for another minute. Remove the dish from the heat and sprinkle with the sesame seeds. Serve hot.

PREP TIP: I portion leftover cooked rice into individual servings and keep them in the freezer so they're convenient for making fried rice later. I prefer to use thawed cooked rice because it makes wonderful fried rice that is less sticky, but you can also make this dish with freshly made rice.

PER SERVING: Calories: 338; Total fat: 12g; Saturated fat: 1g; Carbohydrates: 50g; Sugar: 3g; Protein: 6g; Calcium: 47mg

杂豆饭 MIXED BEAN RICE

Beans and rice cooked together form a source of complete protein. Mixed bean rice is popular in Chinese cuisine and valued as a health food. When using whole grains, it's important to soak and cook them properly to eliminate the antinutrients in the rice and beans that block the absorption of their vitamins and minerals. Serve this healthy dish as an alternative to white rice.

PREP TIME:
5 minutes,
plus 8 hours
or up to
2 days to soak

COOK TIME:
50 minutes

³/₄ cup medium-grain
brown rice

¹/₄ cup dried black-eyed peas

¹/₄ cup dried red beans

¹/₄ cup dried black beans

2 cups water

1. In a medium bowl, combine the brown rice, black-eyed peas, red beans, and black beans. Cover them with enough water to double the volume in the bowl, and soak everything for a minimum of 8 hours. Once the rice and beans are soaked, rinse and drain them well.

2. In a medium pot, combine the soaked rice and beans with 2 cups of water. Bring them to a boil over high heat. Reduce the heat to medium-low, cover the pot, and simmer for about 40 minutes, or until all the water is completely absorbed.

3. Serve hot.

PREP TIP: If you can, soak the ingredients for longer, up to 2 days, to allow the rice and beans to germinate. Change the soaking water every 8 to 12 hours. Sprouted whole grains are more nutritious and easier to digest.

PER SERVING: Calories: 164; Total fat: 1g; Saturated fat: 0g; Carbohydrates: 32g; Sugar: 1g; Protein: 7g; Calcium: 24mg

炸酱面 FRIED SAUCE NOODLES

This famous noodle dish, called zhajiang mian in Mandarin, is from my hometown of Beijing. Every family makes it differently, but it is always, without fail, very tasty. The dish is traditionally made with pork, but I have adapted this "fried sauce" to make it vegan.

PREP TIME:
10 minutes

COOK TIME:
20 minutes

1/4 cup canola oil

1 cup (5 1/2 oz / 160g) five-spiced dried (pressed) tofu, cut into 1/4-inch cubes

1 scallion, thinly sliced

1 cup yellow soybean paste

2/3 cup tianmian sauce

4 cups (10 1/2 oz / 300g) bean sprouts

4 cups (7oz / 200g) thin strips of flat Taiwanese cabbage, green cabbage, or napa cabbage

2 medium carrots, finely julienned

1 pound (454g) dried Chinese wheat noodles

2 tablespoons sesame oil

1 large English cucumber, finely julienned

1. In a wok or large skillet, heat the canola oil over medium heat. Add the pressed tofu and scallion and stir for 1 minute. Add the soybean paste and tianmian sauce and fry for 5 minutes, stirring constantly to prevent burning and adjusting the heat so the sauce is just bubbling. (You may add a small amount of water if the sauce is too thick for your liking.) Set the sauce aside.

2. Bring a large pot of water to a boil over high heat. Add the bean sprouts and boil them for 2 1/2 minutes, then scoop them out of the pot and drain them. Add the cabbage to the pot and boil it for 2 1/2 minutes, then drain. Add the carrot to the pot and boil it for 1 1/2 minutes, then drain. Set each vegetable in its own bowl.

3. Add the noodles to the same pot of boiling water and cook them according to the directions on their package. Drain the noodles and transfer them to a separate large bowl. Add the sesame oil to the noodles and mix well (this will prevent the noodles from sticking).

4. Serve the cucumber, cabbage, bean sprouts, carrot, noodles, and sauce all in separate dishes and let everyone top their noodles with as much sauce and toppings as they like. Mix before eating.

INGREDIENT TIP: This recipe uses the regular yellow soybean paste that comes in a form of a sauce (see page 10). If you can only find the dry yellow soybean paste, dilute it with water first before using it.

VARIATION: If you like a spicy kick, use some doubanjiang to replace an equal amount of either the soybean paste or the tianmian sauce. The soybean paste adds saltiness, the tianmian sauce adds sweetness, and the doubanjiang is both salty and spicy. Play with the proportions of the three sauces to create the flavor you desire.

PER SERVING: Calories: 561; Total fat: 18g; Saturated fat: 2g; Carbohydrates: 78g; Sugar: 14g; Protein: 21g; Calcium: 127mg

蔬菜炒米粉 VEGETABLE STIR-FRIED VERMICELLI

Rice vermicelli is popular in southern Chinese cuisine and most well known in Fujian Province. It can be stir-fried with vegetables in just minutes and served as a full meal or a side dish. My children love the simple flavor of this dish and eat all the vegetables entangled in the noodles. I chose common vegetables for this recipe, but the method is very flexible, and you can use any seasonal vegetables you like.

PREP TIME:
10 minutes,
plus
30 minutes to
rehydrate

COOK TIME:
10 minutes

7 ounces (200g) dried rice vermicelli, soaked in cool water for 30 minutes

3 tablespoons canola oil

2 teaspoons red Sichuan peppercorns

1 medium carrot, finely julienned

1/2 large onion, thinly sliced

4 cups (10 1/2 oz / 300g) bean sprouts

1 medium zucchini, finely julienned

2 tablespoons Chinese light soy sauce

1 teaspoon granulated sugar

1/2 teaspoon sea salt

1. Drain the vermicelli well. Using a pair of scissors, cut the vermicelli into 6-inch lengths.

2. In a wok or large nonstick skillet, heat the oil and Sichuan peppercorns over medium heat. Fry the peppercorns for about 3 minutes, or until they are dark brown and fragrant. Discard the peppercorns, leaving the flavored oil in the wok.

3. Add the carrot and onion to the wok and stir for 1 minute. Increase the heat to high, then add the bean sprouts and zucchini and stir for 2 minutes. Add the vermicelli, soy sauce, sugar, and salt. Stir for 2 minutes.

4. Serve hot.

PREP TIP: Cutting the vermicelli shorter ensures that the noodles will mix well with the vegetables instead of being tangled up on their own in clumps.

PER SERVING: Calories: 327; Total fat: 12g; Saturated fat: 1g; Carbohydrates: 52g; Sugar: 7.5g; Protein: 6g; Calcium: 39mg

芝麻酱面 SESAME SAUCE NOODLES

Here is another popular noodle dish from northern China. This is the type of thing you can get at the night markets and food courts. It is simple, refreshing, and satisfying. You can make this dish in advance and keep the noodles, sauces, and chopped vegetables separately in the refrigerator, then combine them before eating.

PREP TIME:
10 minutes

COOK TIME:
10 minutes

10½ ounces (300g) dried Chinese wheat noodles (see Tip)

2 tablespoons sesame oil

¼ cup Chinese sesame paste

1 teaspoon sea salt

6 tablespoons water

6 garlic cloves, minced

6 tablespoons black vinegar

3 tablespoons Chinese light soy sauce

1 teaspoon granulated sugar

1 large English cucumber, finely julienned

½ cup chopped fresh cilantro

1. Bring a large pot of water to a boil over high heat. Add the dried noodles and cook them according to the directions on their package. Immediately drain the noodles in a colander and rinse them under cold water until cooled. Drain well.

2. Place the noodles in a large dish and toss them with the sesame oil (this will prevent the noodles from sticking together).

3. In a small bowl, mix the sesame paste, salt, and water to make a sauce. In another small bowl, mix the garlic, vinegar, soy sauce, and sugar, stirring to dissolve the sugar.

4. To serve, divide the noodles among four bowls and drizzle them with equal amounts of the sesame sauce and the garlic-vinegar sauce. Top each bowl with one-quarter of the julienned cucumber and chopped cilantro. Mix everything together just before eating.

INGREDIENT TIP: For this dish, I use medium-thickness round white wheat noodles. Fresh noodles are ideal but not always available at grocery stores. Most likely, you will have to use dried noodles. If you can't find medium-thickness round white wheat noodles, you can use thin flat white wheat noodles or buckwheat noodles.

PER SERVING: Calories: 442; Total fat: 16g; Saturated fat: 2g; Carbohydrates: 62g; Sugar: 2.5g; Protein: 10g; Calcium: 186mg

豆角焖面 GREEN BEAN–BRAISED NOODLES

This dish brings back childhood memories, as my mother made it often. Braising is a unique noodle preparation method that is common in northern Chinese cuisine but rarely seen anywhere else. Typically, this dish contains fatty pork slices, but I have made it without for this recipe; the noodles and green beans are plenty tasty all on their own when infused with the aromatic spices and garlic.

PREP TIME:
5 minutes

COOK TIME:
15 minutes

10½ ounces (300g) dried Chinese wheat noodles (see Tip)

6 tablespoons canola oil

1 tablespoon red Sichuan peppercorns

1 scallion, thinly sliced on the diagonal

4 cups halved green beans (1lb / 454g)

3 tablespoons Chinese light soy sauce

2 teaspoons dark soy sauce

1 teaspoon sea salt

1 teaspoon granulated sugar

½ teaspoon five-spice powder

1 cup water

10 garlic cloves, minced

1. Bring a large pot of water to a boil over high heat. Add the dried noodles and cook for about 3 minutes, or until the noodles have softened but are still hard in the center. Drain.

2. In a wok or large nonstick skillet, heat the oil over medium heat. Add the Sichuan peppercorns and fry them for about 2 minutes, or until they are browned and fragrant. Discard the peppercorns, leaving the flavored oil in the wok.

3. Increase the heat to medium-high, add the scallion and green beans, and stir for 1½ minutes. Add the light soy sauce, dark soy sauce, salt, sugar, and five-spice powder and stir for 1½ minutes. Add the water and cook the green beans for 2 minutes, stirring occasionally.

4. Using a ladle, remove about half of the broth from the wok and keep it off to the side in a bowl. Spread the noodles into the wok, on top of the green beans, then pour the broth from the bowl over the noodles. Use a pair of chopsticks to separate the noodles and spread them into an even layer.

5. Reduce the heat to medium, cover the wok, and simmer the green beans and noodles for about 7 minutes, or until the water is mostly reduced. Add the garlic and mix everything together. If there is still broth left in the wok, cook everything a little longer, uncovered, to reduce the liquid.

6. Serve hot.

INGREDIENT TIP: For this dish, I use a wide flat dried wheat noodle, because if the noodles are too thin, they won't hold up during the braising. Choose either a round or flat noodle of medium thickness or thicker. If you can find fresh noodles, skip step 1.

PER SERVING: Calories: 494; Total fat: 23g; Saturated fat: 1.5g; Carbohydrates: 65g; Sugar: 5g; Protein: 9g; Calcium: 69mg

四川担担面 SICHUAN DAN DAN NOODLE SOUP

Dan dan noodles, from Sichuan Province, is traditionally a dry-mixed noodle dish sold as a snack. Some cooks like to make this dish with a soup base, and I find this more satisfying as a full meal. A good bowl of dan dan noodles doesn't require a lot of ingredients, but the preserved mustard greens are a must. Although ground meat is often added, you won't miss it in this vegan version.

PREP TIME:
10 minutes

COOK TIME:
10 minutes

2 tablespoons Chinese sesame paste

2 tablespoons sesame oil

4 tablespoons Sichuan Chili Oil (page 110) or store-bought chili oil, plus more for drizzling

6 tablespoons Chinese light soy sauce

2 tablespoons black vinegar

12 (4-inch) baby bok choy (10½ oz / 300g)

10½ ounces (300g) dried Chinese wheat noodles

¾ cup preserved mustard greens (sui mi ya cai)

½ cup sliced scallion

1. In a small bowl, mix the sesame paste and sesame oil to make a sauce.

2. Set up four large soup bowls: Put 1 tablespoon of the sesame sauce, 1 tablespoon of Sichuan chili oil, 1½ tablespoons of light soy sauce, and ½ tablespoon of black vinegar into each bowl.

3. Bring a large pot of water to a boil over high heat. Add the baby bok choy and cook it for 3 minutes. Using a spider strainer or slotted spoon, remove the bok choy and set it aside.

4. Add the noodles to the same pot and boil them according to the directions on their package until al dente. Remove the pot from the heat.

5. As soon as the noodles are ready, pour 1 cup of hot noodle-boiling water into each soup bowl to make the soup base. Drain the noodles and divide them among the bowls.

6. Top each bowl with baby bok choy, 3 tablespoons of the preserved mustard greens, and 2 tablespoons of scallions. Serve hot with more chili oil, if you like.

PER SERVING: Calories: 549; Total fat: 23g; Saturated fat: 2.5g; Carbohydrates: 75g; Sugar: 7.5g; Protein: 11g; Calcium: 219mg

红葱酥蔬菜咸粥
SAVORY VEGETABLE CONGEE WITH CRISPY SHALLOTS

Savory congee is very popular in the south of China and is often made for breakfast. It is healthy but also flavorful, especially when topped with crunchy peanuts and crispy shallots. I've added bok choy to this recipe, but you can incorporate any fresh vegetables you have on hand.

PREP TIME:
5 minutes

COOK TIME:
45 minutes

5 cups water

1/2 cup medium-grain white rice

3 tablespoons canola oil

1 medium shallot (1oz / 25g), thinly sliced

3 cups (7oz / 200g) bok choy, quartered lengthwise and cut into 1/2-inch pieces

1 1/2 teaspoons sea salt

1/4 teaspoon ground white pepper

1/3 cup roasted peanuts (any papery skins removed)

1. In a medium pot, bring the water and rice to a boil over high heat. Reduce the heat to medium-low and simmer the rice for 30 minutes, stirring occasionally.

2. Meanwhile, in a wok or skillet, heat the oil and shallot over low heat and fry the shallot for 4 to 5 minutes, until it is crispy and slightly golden. Remove the shallot from the wok immediately to stop it from further browning. Set both the shallot and the shallot frying oil aside.

3. Stir the bok choy into the pot of rice and season the mixture with the salt and white pepper. Increase the heat to high and bring the rice to a boil. Reduce the heat to medium-low and simmer everything for 5 minutes.

4. To serve, divide the congee among four bowls. Dividing evenly, top each bowl with the peanuts, shallot, and shallot oil.

VARIATION: Try this congee with other leafy vegetables, such as Chinese mustard greens, yu choy, or napa cabbage. Or mix it up with corn, mushrooms, or carrots.

PER SERVING: Calories: 273; Total fat: 17g; Saturated fat: 1.5g; Carbohydrates: 26g; Sugar: 2g; Protein: 6g; Calcium: 65mg

南瓜小米粥 PUMPKIN MILLET CONGEE

It's no surprise that this healthy, delicious congee is a popular breakfast item in China. Both millet and pumpkin are extremely nutritious, and everyone, including kids, loves the dish's sweet taste and soft texture. You often see this congee on restaurant menus, but it is easy to make at home. Small sugar pumpkins are best, but you can also use a larger pumpkin; when pumpkins are out of season, substitute butternut squash, kabocha squash, or sweet potatoes. Note that it's important to very thinly slice the pumpkin so it can dissolve into the congee as it cooks.

PREP TIME:
5 minutes

COOK TIME:
55 minutes

1/3 cup Chinese millet, rinsed (see Tip)

3 cups (14oz / 400g) thinly sliced peeled sugar pumpkin

5 cups water

Brown sugar, for serving

1. In a medium pot, combine the millet, pumpkin, and water. Bring the mixture to a boil over high heat. Reduce the heat to medium-low, cover the pot, and simmer the congee for 45 minutes, or until the pumpkin partially disintegrates into the millet. (Stir occasionally to prevent sticking, and monitor the heat to make sure the pot doesn't overflow.)

2. Serve the congee hot as a breakfast, sprinkled with brown sugar to taste.

INGREDIENT TIP: The varieties of millet grown in China are creamy, soft, and sweet. You won't achieve the same texture and flavor if you use the North American millet found in major supermarkets. If you can't find Chinese (foxtail) millet, you can use roughly half American millet and half rolled oats or glutinous rice to create a congee with a similarly creamy texture, but keep in mind the flavor will not be the same.

VARIATION: To make your congee fancier, try adding some jujubes and goji berries. Jujubes can be cooked in the congee from the beginning, but goji berries should be added 5 to 10 minutes before the cooking is done.

PER SERVING: Calories: 112; Total fat: 0.5g; Saturated fat: 0g; Carbohydrates: 25g; Sugar: 6.5g; Protein: 3g; Calcium: 33mg

八宝粥 EIGHT TREASURE CONGEE

This special congee is traditionally eaten on the eighth day of the twelfth lunar month to celebrate a big Buddhist festival called la ba jie. The eight treasures originally indicated eight different ingredients, but over time this congee has evolved to incorporate way more ingredients than eight. Each region, family, and person makes this dish differently. My version is a combination of ingredients more commonly available in North American Chinese markets.

PREP TIME:
5 minutes, plus 8 hours to up to 2 days to soak

COOK TIME:
1 hour 20 minutes

1/4 cup black rice (Forbidden Rice)

1/4 cup dried mung beans

1/4 cup dried red beans

1/4 cup glutinous rice

10 cups water

1/2 cup lotus seeds

1 cup (5oz /140g) 1/2-inch cubes taro

1/2 cup roughly chopped walnuts

1/2 cup raisins

Brown sugar, for serving

1. In a medium bowl, combine the black rice, mung beans, and red beans. Cover them with enough water to double the volume in the bowl and soak everything for a minimum of 8 hours to properly rehydrate. (See the Prep Tip on page 71 if you want to make the ingredient more nutritious.) At the same time, in a small bowl, soak the glutinous rice in at least ½ cup of water for 4 to 12 hours.

2. Drain the two bowls of rice and beans and transfer everything to a large pot.

3. Add 10 cups of water, the lotus seeds, taro, walnuts, and raisins to the pot. Bring everything to a boil over high heat. Reduce the heat to medium-low, cover the pot, and simmer the congee for 1 hour 10 minutes, stirring occasionally to prevent sticking.

4. Serve hot, sprinkled with brown sugar to taste.

INGREDIENT TIP: The glutinous rice typically found in the market is refined glutinous rice, meaning it has had its germ removed. It doesn't take as much time to soak, but it will also not germinate. If you use a whole-grain glutinous rice, just soak it for the same amount of time and in the same bowl with the black rice (which is typically a whole-grain rice) and beans.

PER SERVING: Calories: 253; Total fat: 7g; Saturated fat: 0.5g; Carbohydrates: 43g; Sugar: 12g; Protein: 7g; Calcium: 46mg

Celery-Tofu Pot Stickers . **PAGE 88**

6

Dumplings, Rolls, and Small Bites

饺子皮 DUMPLING WRAPPERS

Homemade dumpling wrappers are 100-percent better than store-bought ones. It's not as daunting a task as you might think to make your own; you only need two ingredients and a little practice. I've been rolling dumpling wrappers every Sunday since I was 10. If I could do it then, you can do it now. Make them only when you are ready to wrap dumplings, not ahead of time. If you want to prepare the dough ahead of time, you can refrigerate it in plastic wrap overnight and roll the wrappers out right before you use them.

PREP TIME:
45 minutes, plus 2 to 4 hours to rest

2 cups all-purpose flour, plus more for dusting

2/3 cup room-temperature water, plus more if needed

SPECIAL EQUIPMENT:
Dumpling rolling pin

1. Put the flour in a bowl. Gradually add the water while stirring quickly with a pair of chopsticks, to form lumps. Using your hands, press the lumps into a dough. If the dough is too dry, add 1 to 2 teaspoons more water. Knead the dough for 5 minutes. Cover the dough with a damp towel and let it rest for 2 to 4 hours.

2. Cut the dough in half. Put half back under the damp towel. Squeeze the other half into a long rope about the thickness of a quarter.

3. Dust the cutting board with flour. Cut the rope into small pieces about the size of a cherry (8 to 10g each), and as you cut, roll the rope forward on the cutting board 90 degrees between the first and second cut, then backward between the second and third cut (to prevent the small dough pieces from sticking together and to give them a more rounded shape). Repeat with the remaining dough. Dust the pieces with more flour. Set each piece on one of its cut surfaces and press it down with the palm of your hand to flatten it a bit.

4. Working with one piece at a time, roll out the wrappers, using one hand to work the rolling pin and one hand to turn the wrapper as you roll. With the rolling pin, first flatten just the edges of the wrapper, rolling from the outside of the edge closest to you toward the center, then rotate the disk counterclockwise just a bit to repeat the process on the next side of the wrapper. Continue rolling the edges and rotating the wrapper until the entire piece is flattened and the wrapper is about 2½ inches in diameter.

5. Repeat with remaining dough. Use immediately.

PREP TIP: The ideal way to measure the ingredients for this dough is to weigh both the flour and water. The weight of water should be somewhere between 50 percent and 55 percent of the weight of the flour. This guarantees a firm dough, which is easier to roll.

PER SERVING (4 OUNCES/12 TO 15 WRAPPERS): Calories: 227; Total fat: 0.5g; Saturated fat: 0g; Carbohydrates: 48g; Sugar: 0g; Protein: 6g; Calcium: 9mg

油菜香菇粉丝饺子
YU CHOY, SHIITAKE, AND GLASS NOODLE DUMPLINGS

Dumplings are popular in Northern China. In vegetable dumplings, shiitake mushrooms and glass noodles are often used to create a meaty flavor and texture. You can use a food processor to chop the vegetables if you want to speed up the process.

PREP TIME:
45 minutes, plus 2 hours or up to overnight to rehydrate

COOK TIME:
20 minutes

16 medium dried shiitake mushrooms (1¹/₂ oz / 40g), soaked in cool water for 2 hours or up to overnight

2 cups (8¹/₂ oz / 240g) finely chopped yu choy

1 bunch (1¹/₂ oz / 40g) glass noodles, soaked in cool water for 15 minutes

1 tablespoon sesame oil

2 teaspoons minced fresh ginger

1³/₄ teaspoons sea salt

¹/₄ teaspoon ground white pepper

Dumpling Wrappers (page 84) or 1 pound (454g) store-bought dumpling wrappers

Black vinegar or Dumpling Dipping Sauce (page 111), for serving

1. Discard the tough stems from the shiitakes. Squeeze out as much water as possible from the caps and finely chop them. In a large bowl, combine the shiitake and the yu choy.

2. Drain the noodles and pat them dry. Using scissors, cut the noodles into ½-inch segments. Add the noodles to the bowl. Add the sesame oil, ginger, salt, and white pepper and mix well.

3. Fill and fold the dumpling wrappers using the pleated crescent fold (see page 7).

4. Boil or steam the dumplings, in batches:

   To boil the dumplings: Bring a pot of water to a boil over high heat. Drop a few dumplings into the water without crowding the pot. Using a ladle, move the dumplings gently to prevent sticking. When the pot returns to a boil, reduce the heat to medium to maintain a constant boil. Boil the dumplings for 5 minutes, then remove them from the water using a spider strainer or slotted spoon.

   To steam the dumplings: Line a bamboo steamer with a round of parchment paper or some cabbage leaves. Place the dumplings in the steamer with 1 inch between them. Bring the steamer to full steam over high heat, then reduce the heat to medium and steam the dumplings for 10 minutes.

5. Serve the dumplings hot with black vinegar or dumpling dipping sauce.

PER SERVING: Calories: 338; Total fat: 4g; Saturated fat: 0.5g; Carbohydrates: 66g; Sugar: 0.5g; Protein: 9g; Calcium: 152mg

芹菜豆腐锅贴 CELERY-TOFU POT STICKERS

Pot stickers are panfried dumplings. My kids could eat them every day. This celery and tofu filling is simple yet delicious and creates a nice contrast to the crispy panfried wrapper.

PREP TIME:
45 minutes

COOK TIME:
30 minutes

10¹/₂ ounces (300g) extra-firm tofu, drained

5 large celery stalks (10¹/₂ oz / 300g)

2 tablespoons sesame oil

1¹/₂ teaspoons sea salt

¹/₂ teaspoon granulated sugar

Dumpling Wrappers (page 84) or 1 pound (454g) store-bought dumpling wrappers

Canola oil, for pan-frying

Black vinegar or Dumpling Dipping Sauce (page 111), for serving

1. Squeeze out as much excess water as possible from the tofu. In a bowl, crumble the tofu with your hands into a texture similar to ground meat.

2. Remove the tough strings of the celery stalks by snapping the stalks in half and peeling off any remaining intact strings.

3. Set up a bowl of cold water. Bring a medium pot of water to a boil over high heat. Add the celery and boil it for 4 minutes, or until it is tender. Immediately transfer the celery to the cold water to cool. Drain the celery and squeeze out as much excess water as possible.

4. Finely chop the celery, and add it to the bowl of tofu along with the sesame oil, salt, and sugar, and stir well to combine.

5. Fill and fold the dumplings using the pleated crescent fold (see page 7).

6. Working in batches, in a large nonstick skillet, heat 1 tablespoon of canola oil over medium heat. Place the dumplings in the pan, leaving ½ inch of space between them. Add ½ cup of water to the pan, then cover the pan and cook the dumplings for about 7 minutes, or until all the water evaporates. (If the water evaporates too quickly, add a little more.) When the bottoms of the dumplings turn crispy and golden yellow, remove them from the pan. Repeat this process to cook the remaining dumplings, using 1 tablespoon of the oil and ½ cup of water per batch.

7. Serve hot with vinegar or dumpling dipping sauce.

PER SERVING: Calories: 511; Total fat: 25g; Saturated fat: 2.5g; Carbohydrates: 53g; Sugar: 2.5g; Protein: 14g; Calcium: 94mg

AT 6 SERVINGS: PER SERVING: Calories: 341; Total fat: 17g; Saturated fat: 2g; Carbohydrates: 35g; Sugar: 2g; Protein: 9g; Calcium: 63mg

红油抄手 SICHUAN CHILI OIL WONTONS

These tasty wontons in warm spicy broth are a famous snack from Sichuan Province. These wontons traditionally have a pork filling, but my vegan version uses flavored mushrooms and tofu. I hope you love it as much as I do.

PREP TIME:
45 minutes, plus 2 hours or up to overnight to rehydrate

COOK TIME:
30 minutes

¼ cup (¼ oz / 7g) wood ear mushrooms, soaked in cool water for 2 to 4 hours

4 dried shiitake mushrooms (⅓ oz / 10g), soaked in cool water for 2 hours or up to overnight

½ cup (3oz / 80g) roughly chopped five-spiced dried (pressed) tofu

1 tablespoon vegetarian oyster sauce

5 tablespoons Chinese light soy sauce, divided

1 (8oz / 227gram) package store-bought wonton wrappers

4 tablespoons black vinegar

4 tablespoons Sichuan Chili Oil (page 110) or store-bought chili oil

4 teaspoons granulated sugar

4 teaspoons sesame oil

2 teaspoons red Sichuan peppercorn powder

4 tablespoons chopped fresh cilantro

1 scallion, thinly sliced

1. Bring a large pot of water to a boil over high heat. Add the wood ear mushrooms and boil them for 7 minutes. Remove them from the water using a spider strainer or slotted spoon. (Keep the pot of water on standby.)

2. Meanwhile, discard the shiitake stems. Squeeze the excess water from the caps and then roughly chop them.

3. In a food processor, combine the wood ear mushroom, shiitake, dried tofu, oyster sauce, and 1 tablespoon of the soy sauce and process everything until it's finely chopped.

4. Using the wonton wrappers, fill and fold the wontons (see page 8).

5. Prepare four soup bowls: Put 1 tablespoon of soy sauce, 1 tablespoon of vinegar, 1 tablespoon of Sichuan chili oil, 1 teaspoon of sugar, 1 teaspoon of sesame oil, ½ teaspoon of Sichuan peppercorn powder, 1 tablespoon of cilantro, and one-quarter of the sliced scallion in each.

6. Reheat the pot of water over high heat to bring it to a boil. Add the wontons and gently push them around with a ladle to prevent sticking. When the water comes back to a boil, reduce the heat to medium and cook the wontons for 5 minutes.

7. Pour ¼ cup of the hot wonton cooking water into each bowl. Lift the wontons out of the water with a spider strainer or slotted spoon and divide them among the bowls.

PER SERVING: Calories: 370; Total fat: 18g; Saturated fat: 2g; Carbohydrates: 42g; Sugar: 9g; Protein: 9g; Calcium: 85mg

春饼 SPRING PANCAKES

Known to most people as the pancakes served with Beijing duck, these spring pancakes are also served with stir-fries. There is a custom of eating stir-fried dishes wrapped in spring pancakes on the "beginning of spring" day in the traditional Chinese lunar calendar. I recommend serving spring pancakes with the Stir-Fried Bean Sprouts with Asian Chives (page 47).

PREP TIME:
25 minutes, plus
1 hour to rest

COOK TIME:
20 minutes

2¼ cups all-purpose flour, plus more for dusting

1 cup hot water

1 tablespoon canola oil

1. Place the flour in a medium bowl. Pour the hot water into the bowl while stirring quickly with a pair of chopsticks, to form lumps. Press the dough together, and knead the dough inside the bowl for 2 minutes. Cover the dough with a damp towel and let it rest for 1 hour.

2. Dust a work surface with flour. Cut the dough in half and keep one half under the damp towel. Roll one half of the dough into a rope, then cut it into 10 equal pieces. Repeat with the other half of the dough. Press each piece into a flat round using the palm of your hand.

3. Brush a little oil on top of each piece of dough. Sprinkle a pinch of flour onto the oiled side of one piece of dough, then place another piece on top of the first one, oiled-side down. Press the pieces together, then use a rolling pin to flatten them into a thin pancake about 6 inches in diameter.

4. Heat a large dry skillet or griddle over medium heat. Add a pancake and cook it for 1 minute on each side, until it is slightly golden yellow and puffed up but still soft. Repeat to make 10 pancakes.

5. Transfer the cooked pancakes to a plate. Peel the two layers of each pancake apart to make a total of 20 individual pancakes. Serve immediately.

PER SERVING: Calories: 287; Total fat: 4g; Saturated fat: 0.5g; Carbohydrates: 54g; Sugar: 0g; Protein: 7g; Calcium: 10mg

素春卷 VEGETABLE SPRING ROLLS

This traditional snack is common across China. Besides vegetable fillings, there are meat and sweet fillings, too. No matter how you stuff them, they are a tasty crunchy treat.

PREP TIME:
5 minutes, plus 2 hours or up to overnight to rehydrate

COOK TIME:
35 minutes

16 medium dried shiitake mushrooms (1½ oz / 40g), soaked in cool water for 2 hours or up to overnight

2 tablespoons canola oil, plus more for deep-frying

1 cup (4½ oz / 130g) tightly packed shredded carrot

1 cup (3oz / 90g) tightly packed shredded Taiwanese flat cabbage or green cabbage

1 cup (2½ oz / 75g) tightly packed bean sprouts

1½ teaspoons sea salt

1 teaspoon granulated sugar

20 (5-inch) square spring roll wrappers

1. Discard the tough stems from the shiitake. Squeeze out as much water as possible from the caps and finely chop them.

2. In a wok or skillet, heat 2 tablespoons of oil over medium-high heat. Add the shiitake, carrot, cabbage, bean sprouts, salt, and sugar and cook, stirring, for 4 minutes.

3. Divide the vegetables into 20 equal portions. Place a spring roll wrapper on the work surface with a corner facing you, like a diamond. Put a portion of the filling horizontally in the middle of the wrapper to form a 3-by-1-inch log. Fold the bottom corner up around the log. Fold the left and right corners toward the middle to wrap the filling tightly, then roll the log to wrap the spring roll. Wet the top corner and stick it to the wrapper. Repeat with the remaining wrappers and filling.

4. In a deep pot, heat at least 3 inches of oil over medium-high heat. When a wooden chopstick lowered into the oil immediately sizzles (350ºF), the oil is ready. Working with only a few at a time, gently lower the spring rolls into the oil. Turning them occasionally with chopsticks to fry both sides, fry the spring rolls for 3 to 4 minutes, until crispy and golden.

PER SERVING (1 SPRING ROLL): Calories: 144; Total fat: 10g; Saturated fat: 1g; Carbohydrates: 11g; Sugar: 1g; Protein: 1g; Calcium: 4mg

葱油饼 SCALLION PANCAKES

The simplest foods are sometimes the best. All we need is a little oil, salt, and scallion to flavor these thin flatbreads. They are soft and crispy, with flaky layers. You can nibble them on their own or use these popular pancakes in place of rice. They pair well with any dish.

PREP TIME:
25 minutes, plus
30 minutes to rest

COOK TIME:
35 minutes

2¼ cups all-purpose flour, plus 2 tablespoons

1½ teaspoons sea salt, divided

1 cup hot water

8 tablespoons canola oil, divided

4 scallions, thinly sliced

1. In a medium bowl, mix 2¼ cups of the flour and ½ teaspoon of the salt. Add the hot water while stirring quickly with a pair of chopsticks to form lumps. Add 1 tablespoon of oil to the bowl and mix. Using your hands, knead the dough in the bowl for 2 minutes. Cover the dough with a damp towel and let it rest for 15 minutes.

2. Meanwhile, in a heatproof medium bowl, combine the scallions and the remaining 1 teaspoon of salt. In a skillet, heat 6 tablespoons of oil over high heat until it just begins to smoke. Immediately pour the hot oil over the scallions in the bowl. Add the remaining 2 tablespoons of flour to the scallions and oil and stir to combine.

3. Rub a thin layer of oil on a cutting board. Cut the dough into 8 equal pieces. Cover it with a damp towel. Working with one piece at a time, use a rolling pin to flatten a piece of dough into a 5-by-12-inch rectangle no more than ⅛ inch thick. Spread one-eighth of the scallion mixture over the entire rectangle. Starting at a long side of the rectangle, roll up the dough to form a long thin rope. Take both

ends of the rope (still flat on the cutting board) and spiral each end in toward the center. When the two spirals meet, stack one on top of the other and press them down to make a disk about 1 inch thick and 3 inches in diameter. Transfer the disk to a plate to rest for 15 minutes. Repeat with the remaining dough and filling.

4. Working with one at a time, place a disk on the cutting board, top it with a piece of parchment paper, and use a rolling pin to flatten it to ⅛ to ¼ inch thick (about 7 inches in diameter). Cook the first pancake (see next step) before rolling out the next one.

5. Heat a large dry skillet or griddle over medium-high heat. Place the pancake in the pan and cook it for 1½ to 2 minutes per side, until it is golden and crispy. While the pancake is cooking, roll out the next one. Repeat with the remaining disks. Serve hot.

PER SERVING: Calories: 522; Total fat: 29g; Saturated fat: 2g; Carbohydrates: 58g; Sugar: 0.5g; Protein: 8g; Calcium: 22mg

腐皮卷 BEAN CURD ROLLS

Vegetable-stuffed bean curd rolls are popular in Buddhist and southern Chinese cuisines. You can eat them as soon as they're steamed or panfry them until crisp and slice them to resemble roasted duck or goose.

PREP TIME:
25 minutes, plus 2 hours or up to overnight to rehydrate

COOK TIME:
35 minutes

8 medium dried shiitake mushrooms (³/₄ oz / 20g), soaked in cool water for 2 hours or up to overnight

4 tablespoons canola oil, divided

1 teaspoon minced fresh ginger

1¹/₂ cups (4oz / 120g) finely julienned carrot

1¹/₂ cups (7oz / 200g) finely julienned canned bamboo shoots

3¹/₂ tablespoons Chinese light soy sauce, divided

2 tablespoons Shaoxing wine

¹/₂ teaspoon sea salt

¹/₂ teaspoon granulated sugar, plus 1 tablespoon

1 tablespoon sesame oil

1¹/₂ tablespoons vegetarian oyster sauce

2 tofu skin (yuba) sheets

1 tablespoon cornstarch

¹/₂ teaspoon five-spice powder

SPECIAL EQUIPMENT:
Flat-bottomed stainless steel or bamboo steamer, lined with cheesecloth, with a large pot

1. Drain the mushrooms, reserving 1½ cups of the soaking water. Discard the shiitake stems. Squeeze the caps to remove as much water as possible and thinly slice them.

2. In a wok or large skillet, heat 1 tablespoon of canola oil over medium-high heat. Add the ginger, shiitakes, and carrot and stir for 2 minutes. Add the bamboo shoot, 2 tablespoons of the soy sauce, the wine, salt, and ½ teaspoon of the sugar and stir for 2 minutes. Remove the pan from the heat, then stir in the sesame oil and let the vegetables cool.

3. In a large, deep plate or tray, mix the mushroom soaking water, oyster sauce, the remaining 1½ tablespoons of soy sauce, and the remaining 1 tablespoon of sugar. Stir to dissolve the sugar.

4. Dip 1 sheet of tofu skin in the liquid mixture to soften it for 2 minutes. Squeeze out the excess liquid and lay the tofu skin on a flat surface. Place half of the filling in a horizontal log in the center, near the bottom of the sheet. Fold the bottom of the tofu skin up around the filling as tightly as possible. Fold the extra tofu skin on the sides of the log in toward the middle. Roll the log forward until the tofu skin wraps the log. Repeat to make a second roll.

5. Place the rolls into a steamer lined with cheesecloth (or a dish inside the steamer). Heat the steamer over high heat until it comes to full steam. Reduce the heat to medium and steam for 10 minutes.

6. Meanwhile, transfer the leftover liquid to a small pot. Stir in the cornstarch and five-spice powder. Heat the mixture over high heat, stirring constantly, until it thickens.

7. In a large nonstick skillet, heat the remaining 3 tablespoons of canola oil over medium-high heat. Add the bean curd rolls and fry for 1 to 2 minutes on each side, until golden and crispy.

8. Cut the rolls into 1-inch-thick slices. Arrange the slices on a plate and pour the sauce over top. Serve hot.

PER SERVING: Calories: 275; Total fat: 18g; Saturated fat: 2g; Carbohydrates: 19g; Sugar: 8.5g; Protein: 7g; Calcium: 50mg

紫薯发糕 PURPLE SWEET POTATO SPONGE CAKE

Sponge cakes (fa gao) are traditional leavened steamed breads. They are slightly sweet and suitable for breakfast, snacks, or as a part of a full meal. The color of purple sweet potato makes this sponge cake very appealing, and sweet jujubes add a delicious fruity flavor.

PREP TIME:
15 minutes, plus 2½ to 3½ hours to rest

COOK TIME:
1 hour

1 medium purple sweet potato (4oz / 113g)

²/₃ cup warm water

2 tablespoons granulated sugar

½ teaspoon active dry yeast

1 cup all-purpose flour

½ cup jujubes, pitted and cut into small pieces

SPECIAL EQUIPMENT:
Flat-bottomed stainless steel or bamboo steamer with a large pot

1. Place the sweet potato in a steamer and heat on high. When it comes to a full steam, reduce the heat to medium and steam for 30 minutes. Let the potato cool to room temperature, then peel and mash the flesh until smooth.

2. In a medium bowl, mix the water, sugar, and yeast; let it rest for 15 minutes.

3. Gradually add the flour to the yeast mixture, stirring to make a batter. Add the sweet potato and stir to combine. Stir in the jujubes.

4. Pour the batter into a deep 7- to 8-inch baking dish or cake pan lined with parchment paper and cover it with a large dish placed upside down (or anything that won't touch the batter) to prevent it from drying out. Let the batter rise on the counter for 2 to 3 hours, until it has doubled in size.

5. Place the baking dish in the steamer and heat on high heat. When it comes to a full steam, reduce the heat to medium and steam the cake for 20 minutes. Let the cake cool until you can touch it, then cut it into smaller pieces and serve immediately.

INGREDIENT TIP: If jujubes are not available, skip them or substitute another dried fruit. If you omit the jujubes/dried fruit, you may want to add extra sugar. In the absence of a purple sweet potato, use a regular sweet potato instead.

PER SERVING: Calories: 245; Total fat: 0.5g; Saturated fat: 0g; Carbohydrates: 56g; Sugar: 19g; Protein: 5g; Calcium: 31mg

豆渣玉米窝头 SOY PULP CORNMEAL BUNS

Cornmeal buns (wo tou) are a very traditional country-style bread. Adding soy pulp creates a softer texture while reducing waste from making soy milk. Soy pulp also adds extra nutrients and protein. You can eat these buns as part of a meal in place of rice, and sometimes people put stir-fried dishes inside the buns. I suggest serving these with Black Bean Dried Tofu and Garlic Scapes (page 42).

PREP TIME:
15 minutes

COOK TIME:
35 minutes

1 cup cornmeal (fine or medium grind)

2 tablespoons granulated sugar

1/4 teaspoon baking soda

1/3 cup hot water

1 cup soy pulp (left over from Homemade Soy Milk, page 106)

SPECIAL EQUIPMENT:
Flat-bottomed stainless steel or bamboo steamer with a large pot

1. In a bowl, combine the cornmeal, sugar, and baking soda and mix well.

2. Pour the hot water into the cornmeal mix, stirring quickly with a pair of chopsticks until all the cornmeal binds with the water. Let the batter sit for 3 minutes to cool, until you can safely touch it.

3. Add the soy pulp and massage the mixture until the ingredients form a dough. If the mixture is too dry, add a little hot water. If it's too wet, add a little cornmeal.

4. Divide the dough into 8 equal pieces and shape each piece by hand into a cone. Press a hole into the base of the cone. (This ensures the buns will cook through.)

5. Line a steamer basket with parchment paper. Place the buns into the steamer with 1 inch of space between them. Heat the steamer over high heat until it comes to a full steam. Reduce the heat to medium and steam for 30 minutes.

6. Serve hot.

PREP TIP: Be sure to mix the baking soda well with the cornmeal. If you don't, the cooked cornmeal buns will have dark spots on them.

PER SERVING: Calories: 193; Total fat: 1g; Saturated fat: 0g; Carbohydrates: 41g; Sugar: 7g; Protein: 4g; Calcium: 26mg

酥脆胡萝卜香菜素丸子
CRISPY CARROT-CILANTRO VEGGIE BALLS

Deep-fried veggie balls are a staple of spring festival celebrations in northern China. There are endless variations to this recipe, but they always feature carrots or daikon radish. Using cornstarch and frying the ball twice gives them a crispy texture. These tasty carrot balls are great served as a snack or a side dish.

PREP TIME:
10 minutes

COOK TIME:
10 minutes

3¹/₂ cups (1lb / 454g) finely shredded carrot

1 cup chopped fresh cilantro

2 tablespoons minced fresh ginger

2 tablespoons sliced scallion

2 teaspoons sea salt

¹/₂ teaspoon ground white pepper

¹/₂ teaspoon five-spice powder

2 tablespoons Shaoxing wine

1¹/₂ cups cornstarch

Canola oil, for deep-frying

1. In a medium bowl, mix the carrot, cilantro, ginger, scallion, salt, white pepper, and five-spice powder. Massage the mixture to release the juices from the vegetables. Add the rice wine and cornstarch and mix with your hands.

2. In a deep pot, heat at least 3 inches of oil over medium heat. When a wooden chopstick lowered into the oil immediately sizzles, the oil is ready (350°F).

3. Working in batches, make 1-inch-diameter balls out of the vegetable mixture and gently drop them into the oil. Be careful not to crowd the pot and use chopsticks to prevent sticking. As soon as the balls float to the surface, take them out using a metal spider strainer or slotted spoon. Repeat with the remaining mixture.

4. After all the veggie balls are fried, increase the heat to medium-high. Working in batches again, drop the veggie balls back into the oil and refry them for another 15 seconds to crisp up their surfaces. Serve hot.

PREP TIP: I prefer these veggie balls with the irregular shape they get when the shredded carrots stick out a bit, because they are crispier when fried. To achieve this, don't pack the balls too tight and don't smooth out the surface by rolling them between your palms.

PER SERVING: Calories: 367; Total fat: 14g; Saturated fat: 1g; Carbohydrates: 56g; Sugar: 5.5g; Protein: 1g; Calcium: 45mg

麻辣五香锅巴 CHILI FIVE-SPICE SCORCHED RICE

Before rice cookers, crusty rice would naturally form on the bottom of the rice pot. This crust could be seasoned and turned into a chip-like snack. In my childhood, these crunchy and spicy rice chips were sold in bags in stores. Nowadays, rice cookers make perfect rice every time, so we must go to lengths to re-create this traditional snack, but it's totally worth it!

PREP TIME:
10 minutes

COOK TIME:
35 minutes

3 cups freshly cooked medium-grain rice

1½ teaspoons sea salt

1 teaspoon red Sichuan peppercorn powder

1 teaspoon chili pepper powder

1 teaspoon five-spice powder

1 teaspoon ground cumin

1 teaspoon granulated sugar

¼ cup canola oil

1. Position a rack in the center of the oven and preheat the oven to 350ºF.

2. In a bowl, combine the rice, salt, spices, sugar, and oil. Blend everything by mashing it with a potato masher (or transfer the mixture to a food processer and blend it until the rice is broken into small pieces).

3. Lay a piece of parchment paper the size of a baking sheet on a cutting board. Spread half of the rice in the middle of the parchment and cover it with another piece of parchment paper of the same size. Flatten the mixture with a rolling pin to no more than ⅛ inch thick. Remove the top paper. Dip a knife or a pizza cutter in water, then cut the rice into 1-inch squares, leaving them in place on the parchment paper. Carefully transfer the parchment paper to a baking sheet. Repeat this process with the remaining rice mixture, more parchment paper, and a second baking sheet.

4. Bake the rice for 35 minutes, or until it has crisped up. Remove it and cool for 10 minutes. Break the rice into individual pieces, along the cut lines.

PREP TIP: Leftover rice is drier and harder to work with. If you want to use it, you may need to add a splash of hot water to soften it. The baking time may vary a little depending on the moisture content, thickness, and how crispy you like your rice.

PER SERVING: Calories: 311; Total fat: 14g; Saturated fat: 1g; Carbohydrates: 41g; Sugar: 1.5g; Protein: 3g; Calcium: 8mg

Mung Bean Cakes,
PAGE 114

7

Basics and Desserts

烤麸 STEAMED SEITAN

This Chinese-style seitan (kao fu) is a steamed leavened gluten bread often used in stews and braised dishes, where the spongy texture soaks up flavors and broth. It is the star of the famous dish su shi jin (Assorted Vegetarian Delicacies, page 24). Traditionally, gluten dough was made by washing away the starch from wheat flour dough. Now we can make it from gluten flour in a fraction of time.

PREP TIME:
10 minutes, plus 2 hours 15 minutes to 3 hours 15 minutes to rest

COOK TIME:
40 minutes

²/₃ cup warm water

¼ teaspoon active dry yeast

¼ teaspoon granulated sugar

1 cup vital wheat gluten

SPECIAL EQUIPMENT:
Flat-bottomed stainless steel or bamboo steamer with a large pot

1. In a medium bowl, mix the water, yeast, and sugar. Let it rest for 15 minutes.

2. Add the wheat gluten gradually while stirring quickly with chopsticks to form lumps. If there is still dry flour left, add a little more water. Be careful not to add too much water.

3. Knead the dough for 2 minutes on a flat surface. Stretch the dough into a flat round shape and spread it on a piece of parchment paper. Press the dough to ¾ inch thick. Cover it with a damp kitchen towel to keep moist. Let it rise on the counter for 2 to 3 hours, until the dough has doubled in size.

4. Lift the parchment paper and transfer the dough to the dish you will use in the steamer or directly into the steamer basket.

5. Heat the steamer over high heat until it comes to a full steam. Reduce the heat to medium and steam for 30 minutes. Remove the seitan from the steamer. Use a pair of scissors to cut the seitan into 1-inch cubes.

6. Store the seitan in an airtight container in the refrigerator for 2 days or in the freezer for up to 1 month.

PER SERVING (2OZ / 56 G): Calories: 94; Total fat: 0g; Saturated fat: 0g; Carbohydrates: 8g; Sugar: 0g; Protein: 13g; Calcium: 0mg

油面筋 FRIED GLUTEN BALLS

Fried gluten balls (you mian jin) are from Jiangsu Province. It was said that a nun invented them by accident. Gluten dough naturally expands in hot oil, so you don't need a leavener to make it puff up. Fried gluten balls absorb flavors easily and add a meaty bite to vegan dishes.

PREP TIME:
5 minutes,
plus 1½ hours
to rest

COOK TIME:
40 minutes

1¼ cups water

½ teaspoon sea salt

¾ cup vital wheat gluten

Canola oil, for deep-frying

1. Pour the water into a medium bowl. In a small bowl, mix together the salt and wheat gluten. Sprinkle the wheat gluten mixture into the bowl of water while stirring quickly with chopsticks. Gently massage the dough for 2 minutes in the water until all the gluten flour sticks together, then squeeze out the extra water from the dough. Do not knead. Discard the starchy water.

2. Gently pull the dough into small, round cherry-size pieces. Let them rest on a plate for 1½ hours to relax the gluten.

3. In a deep pot, heat at least 3 inches deep of oil over medium-low heat. When the surface of the oil begins moving slowly (250° to 280°F), carefully add a few of the gluten pieces, not overcrowding the pot, and fry them for 7 to 10 minutes. Using chopsticks to keep them from sticking and the back of a spider strainer or slotted spoon to submerge them in the oil, turn the pieces frequently until they are light yellow and about the size of a plum. Remove the balls using the spider strainer and repeat with the remaining dough.

4. The gluten balls will deflate once cooled. Immediately return them to the oil and fry them again for 2 minutes over medium heat (325° to 350°F). They will expand again and hold their shape once thoroughly cooked. The finished gluten balls should be light golden.

5. Freeze the balls in an airtight container or zip-top bags for up to 3 months.

PER SERVING (1 BALL): Calories: 28; Total fat: 2.5g; Saturated fat: 0g; Carbohydrates: <1g; Sugar: 0g; Protein: 1g; Calcium: 3mg

自制豆浆 HOMEMADE SOY MILK

Soy milk is the traditional breakfast drink in China. Many families make their own on a regular basis. Plain soy milk is also the main ingredient for tofu products.

PREP TIME:
1 hour, plus 12 to 48 hours to soak

COOK TIME:
25 minutes

1 pound (454g) dried soybeans

10 cups water

SPECIAL EQUIPMENT:
Nut milk bag

1. In a large bowl, soak the soybeans in enough water to generously cover for a minimum of 12 hours and up to 2 days. (See the Prep Tip on page 71 to make the soybeans more nutritious.) Change the water every 8 to 12 hours. Make sure the soybeans are completely submerged. Drain and rinse the soybeans.

2. Working in batches, combine the soaked soybeans and the water and puree. Pour the soybean puree into a nut milk bag held over a large pot. Squeeze out as much soy milk as possible into the pot. Discard or repurpose the soy pulp (such as in Soy Pulp Cornmeal Buns, page 99).

3. Bring the pot of soy milk to a boil over high heat, uncovered. Keep a careful eye on the soy milk as it can easily boil over. Once the soy milk comes to a boil, keep it at a constantly boiling temperature without overflowing (around medium heat) for 15 to 20 minutes, stirring frequently.

4. Use a fine-mesh skimmer to remove any foam from the top of the soy milk. Remove the pot from the heat. Store the soy milk in a sealed jar in the refrigerator for up to 1 week.

VARIATION: Though it is tricky and time-consuming, you can also use this recipe to make **tofu skin** and **dried bean curd sticks**: As you boil the soy milk, a thin layer of bean curd will form on the surface. Take that layer out and lay it flat to make tofu skin. A pot of boiling soy milk will continue to produce bean curd layers. To make dried bean curd sticks, hang the skins and let them dry.

PER SERVING (1 CUP): Calories: 131; Total fat: 4g; Saturated fat: 0.5g; Carbohydrates: 15g; Sugar: 9.5g; Protein: 8g; Calcium: 61mg

自制豆腐 TOFU FROM SCRATCH

Tofu is an important ingredient in Chinese cooking, and making your own fresh tofu at home is easy. To make tofu, you need a coagulant. There are four common coagulants. I use gypsum (calcium sulphate) in this recipe.

PREP TIME:
25 minutes, plus time to press

COOK TIME:
10 minutes

8 cups Homemade Soy Milk (page 106) or store-bought soy milk

1 tablespoon gypsum (calcium sulfate)

2 cups water

SPECIAL EQUIPMENT:
Tofu press and cheesecloth

1. In a large pot, bring the soy milk to a boil. Remove from the heat immediately.

2. In a small bowl, dilute the gypsum in the water. Pour the solution into the soy milk. Stir quickly, then let the soy milk sit for 3 to 5 minutes, until curds form and the liquid turns clear.

3. Line a tofu press with cheesecloth. Place the tofu press on a stand over a bowl. Ladle the tofu curds into the mold and smooth them gently with your fingers to fill in the space. Fold the cheesecloth over to wrap the tofu. Place the tofu press cover on top of the tofu.

4. **For extra-firm tofu:** Place a 4-pound weight on the tofu and press for 20 minutes.
   For firm tofu: Use a 3-pound weight for 15 minutes.
   For medium-firm tofu: Use a 2-pound weight for 10 minutes.
   For soft tofu: Use a 1-pound weight for 5 minutes.

5. Let the tofu cool and store in cold water in an airtight container in the refrigerator, changing the water every day, for up to 5 days.

VARIATION TIP: The same process for making tofu can be used to make **fresh bean curd sheets**. Instead of filling the tofu press full, only fill in a thin layer of tofu curds. That said, buying your tofu sheets is far more practical than making them at home, as commercial tofu makers can press much larger sheets at a time.

PER SERVING (4 OZ EXTRA-FIRM): Calories: 163; Total fat: 10g; Saturated fat: 1.5g; Carbohydrates: 3g; Sugar: <1g; Protein: 19g; Calcium: 774mg

豆腐泡 TOFU PUFFS

Deep-fried tofu puffs (dou fu pao) are used in a variety of stir-fries and stews. They are an essential ingredient in vegan Chinese cooking. Store-bought tofu puffs are made from a special type of tofu to create the air pockets and texture and can't be replicated with regular tofu. However, we can mimic tofu puffs at home to the best of our abilities.

PREP TIME:
5 minutes

COOK TIME:
30 minutes

²/₃ block extra-firm Tofu from Scratch (page 107) or 1 (16oz / 454g) package store-bought extra-firm tofu

1 teaspoon sea salt

1 cup water

Canola oil, for deep-frying

1. Cut the tofu into 1- to 1½-inch cubes.

2. In a small bowl, dissolve the salt in the water. Dip the tofu in the salt water, then pat it dry.

3. In a deep pot, heat at least 3 inches of oil over medium-low heat. When the surface of the oil begins moving slowly (250° to 280°F), working in batches, carefully place the tofu cubes into the oil, not overcrowding the pot. Fry for 8 to 10 minutes, until they float. Be patient with frying at low temperatures; if the heat is too high, it will overcook and harden the tofu's surface.

4. Increase the heat to medium-high. Continue frying the tofu for 2 to 3 minutes, until the surface turns a light golden color but is still soft. Remove the tofu using a spider strainer or a slotted spoon.

5. Freeze the tofu puffs in an airtight container or zip-top bag for up to 1 month.

INGREDIENT TIP: Store-bought tofu puffs are made from extra-firm nigari tofu. Nigari is a tofu coagulant also known as magnesium chloride. Nigari tofu is common in northern China, while gypsum (calcium sulphate) tofu is common in southern China. Most tofu sold in North American supermarkets is gypsum tofu, and the nigari tofu sold in stores is often not firm enough to make puffs. Buy the firmest you can find. Freezing the fried tofu will create a spongy texture similar to store-bought tofu puffs.

PER SERVING (1 TOFU PUFF): Calories: 58; Total fat: 4.5g; Saturated fat: 0.5g; Carbohydrates: 1g; Sugar: 0g; Protein: 4g; Calcium: 29mg

素肉 MOCK MEAT

Prepackaged mock meats sold in stores are made from bean curd products boiled in a brine, then rolled up and pressed together. You can totally replicate this "vegetarian chicken" and "vegetarian duck" at home. This recipe is a northern version using fresh bean curd sheets. In the south, rehydrated dried tofu skin (yuba) is often used, but the idea is the same. Serve this with Mock Meat Dipping Sauce (page 112).

PREP TIME:
10 minutes,
plus
20 minutes
to rest

COOK TIME:
25 minutes

1 (11oz / 320g) package fresh bean curd sheets

4 cups water

3 tablespoons Shaoxing wine

2 tablespoons Chinese light soy sauce

2 teaspoons sea salt

1 teaspoon five-spice powder

1/2 teaspoon baking soda

1. Cut the bean curd sheets into strips 2 inches long and ½ inch wide.

2. In a medium pot, combine the water, rice wine, soy sauce, salt, five-spice powder, and baking soda. Add the bean curd strips. Bring the pot to a boil over high heat, then reduce the heat to medium-low. Cover the pot and simmer for 15 minutes, or until the bean curd strips are very soft. (The time may vary slightly depending on the brand of your bean curd.) Thoroughly drain the bean curd strips in a colander.

3. Lay a double layer of 18-inch square cheesecloth on the cutting board. Place the bean curd strips in the middle, then roll them into a log. Wrap the cheesecloth tightly around the bean curd roll. Place a flat heavy object on top, such as a cast-iron skillet. Press the bean curd roll for 20 minutes.

4. Unwrap the cheesecloth. Cut the mock meat into slices to serve. If you're not eating it right away, store the mock meat log in an airtight container in the refrigerator for up to 3 days.

PREP TIP: Adding baking soda to the brine helps to soften the bean curd strips.

PER SERVING: Calories: 161; Total fat: 3g; Saturated fat: 2g; Carbohydrates: 8g; Sugar: 1g; Protein: 20g; Calcium: 87mg

辣椒油 SICHUAN CHILI OIL

Making Sichuan chili oil can be an elaborate process involving a dozen herbs and spices. There are a few different methods for making it, too. This home version is easy to make but has a complex flavor. The chilies will settle in the bottom of the jar. In most recipes, the sediment is used along with the oil—simply stir up the oil and chilies with a spoon and take out the desired amount.

PREP TIME:
2 minutes

COOK TIME:
3 minutes

⅓ cup coarse chili pepper powder

¼ cup fine chili pepper powder

2 tablespoons white sesame seeds

1 teaspoon sea salt

½ teaspoon five-spice powder

2 cups canola oil

1 tablespoon black vinegar

1. In a large heatproof bowl, combine both chili pepper powders, the sesame seeds, the salt, and the five-spice powder.

2. In a saucepan, heat the oil over medium-high heat until it just begins to smoke. Remove the pan from the heat and let it cool off for a minute, until the oil is no longer at its smoke point but still sizzles immediately when a wooden chopstick is put in it (it should be around 380°F).

3. Pour half of the hot oil over the chili pepper mix. It will sizzle. Stir immediately to combine the oil and chili pepper powder. Let the mixture sit for 1 minute, then add the black vinegar for extra aroma. Pour the other half of the hot oil into the mixture. It should sizzle more violently this time. Stir again.

4. Store the chili oil in a sealed glass jar in the pantry for up to 2 months.

INGREDIENT TIP: It's best to use two different varieties of chili peppers in this recipe to create layers of flavors. I use cayenne pepper powder as the fine powder. Sometimes Chinese supermarkets carry coarse chili pepper powders. If you can't find coarse chili pepper powders, simply grind whole dried chili peppers (such as facing heaven peppers, Tianjin peppers, or bird's eye chili) or crushed red pepper flakes into a coarse powder. The combination of fine and coarse chili pepper powders creates the perfect consistency.

PER SERVING (1 TABLESPOON): Calories: 96; Total fat: 10g; Saturated fat: 1g; Carbohydrates: 1g; Sugar: 0g; Protein: 0g; Calcium: 6mg

饺子蘸酱 DUMPLING DIPPING SAUCE

My grandma loves dumplings, and during my childhood we made and ate dumplings every weekend. A good dipping sauce is a must to serve with dumplings, so I'm sharing my favorite dipping sauce recipe here. This garlicky sauce brings together the umami of soy sauce, the aroma of sesame oil, the pungency of black vinegar, and the sweetness of sugar. The recipe is flexible; use it as a base dipping sauce recipe for steamed or boiled dumplings or pot stickers, but feel free to add to or subtract from it.

PREP TIME:
5 minutes

¹/₄ cup black vinegar

6 garlic cloves, finely minced

2 tablespoons Chinese light soy sauce

2 teaspoons sesame oil

1 teaspoon granulated sugar

In a small bowl, combine the black vinegar, garlic, soy sauce, sesame oil, and sugar. Mix all the ingredients together until well combined. Serve fresh.

VARIATION: Depending on the kind of dumplings you are serving this with, sometimes the strong garlicky flavor can overpower the flavor of your dumpling fillings. You can skip the garlic in this recipe to make it a milder dipping sauce. If you like spicy food, add some Sichuan Chili Oil (page 110) to your taste.

PER SERVING: Calories: 52; Total fat: 2.5g; Saturated fat: 0.5g; Carbohydrates: 4g; Sugar: 2g; Protein: <1g; Calcium: 19mg

素肉蘸酱 MOCK MEAT DIPPING SAUCE

This dipping sauce is so flavorful on mock meat. Simply slice the mock meat thinly and warm it up in a steamer. Drizzle the sauce over it, and you won't believe how delicious it is! This dipping sauce is free of garlic and onion to suit practicing Buddhists who avoid alliums.

PREP TIME:
5 minutes

COOK TIME:
1 minute

2 tablespoons finely chopped fresh cilantro

1 tablespoon finely minced fresh ginger

Pinch five-spice powder

2 tablespoons canola oil

2 tablespoons Chinese light soy sauce

1/2 teaspoon granulated sugar

1. In a small heatproof bowl, combine the cilantro, ginger, and five-spice powder.

2. In a skillet or a wok, heat the oil over high heat until it begins to smoke. Immediately pour the hot oil onto the ginger and cilantro. The sizzling oil will release the aroma from the herbs and spices.

3. Add the soy sauce and sugar to the bowl. Stir to combine with a spoon. Serve fresh.

PREP TIP: You want the ginger to be very fine for this dipping sauce. I use a lemon zester to grate the fresh ginger over a bowl, which catches all the ginger juice as well.

VARIATION TIP: If you don't like cilantro, you can replace it with scallion. (If you do, however, the sauce will no longer be suitable for the traditional Chinese Buddhist diet.)

PER SERVING: Calories: 70; Total fat: 7g; Saturated fat: 0.5g; Carbohydrates: 1g; Sugar: 1g; Protein: 0g; Calcium: 12mg

姜糖水豆腐花 TOFU PUDDINGS IN GINGER-SUGAR SYRUP

This is a popular dessert in southern China where it's called dou fu hua. It has a delicate sweet taste that's not overwhelming and is often served with sweet toppings. There is a similar product called dou fu nao in the north, but it is usually served with a savory sauce on top.

PREP TIME:
10 minutes, plus
10 minutes to rest

COOK TIME:
30 minutes

3 cups water, plus 6 tablespoons

1 cup packed light brown sugar

1/3 cup thinly sliced fresh ginger

3 tablespoons cornstarch

3 teaspoons gypsum (calcium sulfate)

8 cups Homemade Soy Milk (page 106) or store-bought soy milk

1. In a small pot, combine 3 cups of water, the brown sugar, and ginger. Bring the mixture to a boil over high heat. Reduce the heat to medium-low, cover the pot, and simmer for 20 minutes.

2. Meanwhile, in each of six bowls, mix together 1½ teaspoons of cornstarch, ½ teaspoon of gypsum, and 1 tablespoon of water.

3. In a large pot, bring the soy milk to a full boil, then immediately remove it from the heat. Pour 1⅓ cups of the hot soy milk into each bowl from a high position with a fast pour, using the force of the liquid to quickly disperse the gypsum. Do not stir. Let the bowls sit undisturbed for 10 minutes, or until the soy milk turns into a pudding. Use a spoon to carefully remove any tofu skin and foam from the surface.

4. Strain the ginger syrup through a fine-mesh sieve (discard the ginger).

5. Serve both the pudding and the syrup either hot or cold. For a cold dessert, keep the pudding and the syrup chilled in the refrigerator. When ready to serve, pour the ginger-sugar syrup to taste over the puddings.

PREP TIP: I prefer making tofu puddings in individual bowls, to preserve the perfect shape, rather than making it in a large pot and then scooping it into bowls.

PER SERVING: Calories: 334; Total fat: 5.5g; Saturated fat: 0.5g; Carbohydrates: 61g; Sugar: 49g; Protein: 11g; Calcium: 664mg

绿豆糕 MUNG BEAN CAKES

Mung bean cakes are a summertime dessert and by tradition are often eaten during the Dragon Boat Festival, which is usually in early summer. There are endless ways to make them, and they can be as simple as this three-ingredient version which is accessible for home cooks while still being authentic.

PREP TIME:
15 minutes, plus 12 hours to soak

COOK TIME:
50 minutes

1½ cups peeled dried mung beans

1 cup granulated sugar

½ cup corn oil, or another very mild-flavored oil

SPECIAL EQUIPMENT:

Flat-bottomed stainless steel or bamboo steamer with a large pot

Moon cake mold

1. Soak the beans for 12 hours or overnight. Drain them completely.

2. Place the beans on a deep plate in a steamer. Heat the steamer over high heat until it comes to full steam. Reduce the heat to medium and steam for 30 minutes. Press a bean between your fingers; if it crumbles, it's cooked.

3. Transfer the beans to a food processor and pulse to break them down into a powder. Transfer to a large bowl. Stir in the sugar and the oil and mix well.

4. Heat a wok or a large nonstick skillet over medium heat. Add the paste to the wok and cook it to dry up excess moisture and dissolve the sugar. Fold it with a spatula constantly to prevent browning, until the paste turns into a dough.

5. Let the dough cool for about 10 minutes. Press a piece of the dough into a moon cake mold to make a small cake (follow the instructions that came with the mold as they can differ in size). Repeat until all of the dough has been used. (If you don't have a moon cake mold, you can use the cups of a silicone baking mold. Or instead of making individual cakes, press the dough into a container to form a block and then cut it into squares.)

6. Serve the cakes either fresh or chilled for a better taste. If you're not eating them right away, store in an airtight container in the refrigerator for up to 3 days.

PER SERVING: Calories: 470; Total fat: 19g; Saturated fat: 2.5g; Carbohydrates: 69g; Sugar: 34g; Protein: 13g; Calcium: 26mg

黑芝麻汤圆 BLACK SESAME RICE BALLS

Known as tang yuan in Chinese, this dessert of sweet dumplings served in a hot soup is the symbolic dish eaten to celebrate the first full moon of the lunar year, as well as to mark the end of the spring festival.

PREP TIME:
50 minutes

COOK TIME:
10 minutes

1/2 cup toasted black sesame seeds

3 tablespoons granu-lated sugar

3 tablespoons coconut oil

1 1/2 cups glutinous rice flour

1/3 cup hot water

1/4 cup room-temperature water (or less)

1. In a high-powered blender, combine the sesame seeds and sugar and process until the oil from the sesame seeds binds with the sugar and turns into a thick paste. Transfer the mixture to a bowl and mix in the coconut oil.

2. Pour the mixture into a zip-top bag and shape it into a rectangular block 1/2 inch thick. Chill it in the freezer for 20 minutes, or until just hardened.

3. Meanwhile, place the glutinous rice flour in a small bowl and gradually pour the hot water into it, stirring with a pair of chopsticks. Add the room-temperature water to the bowl a little at a time, using your hands to mix everything together. Stop adding water when the dough is very soft. Knead the dough until smooth. Let it rest for 10 minutes.

4. Remove the sesame filling from the freezer. Cut it into 32 equal pieces. Roll each piece into a ball. Place the balls on a plate and freeze them for 15 minutes, or until they are completely frozen.

5. Divide the dough into 32 equal pieces. Press a piece into a bowl shape. Place a piece of frozen sesame filling inside, then seal the rice flour wrapper to enclose the filling. Roll the ball between your palms to smooth it. Repeat with the remaining balls.

6. Bring a pot of water to a boil. Working in batches, drop some rice balls into the water and cook for 3 to 4 minutes, stirring, until they float to the surface. Repeat until all the rice balls are cooked. Serve hot with some of the cooking liquid.

PER SERVING: Calories: 443; Total fat: 20g; Saturated fat: 9g; Carbohydrates: 61g; Sugar: 9.5g; Protein: 9g; Calcium: 186mg

拔丝红薯 CANDYFLOSS SWEET POTATO

Candyfloss desserts are popular treats in China. They even show up on dinner tables as a sweet dish. Called ba si hong shu in Chinese, these sweet potatoes coated in sticky caramelized sugar syrup are served hot before the coating completely hardens. Enjoy the fun of this treat by pulling a piece from the plate to create golden sugar strands over a foot long.

PREP TIME:
5 minutes

COOK TIME:
25 minutes

4 medium sweet potatoes (1lb /454g)

3 tablespoons cornstarch

1 tablespoon canola oil, plus more for deep-frying

¹/₂ cup granulated sugar

¹/₄ cup water

1 tablespoon distilled white vinegar

1. Peel and quarter the sweet potatoes lengthwise. Roll-cut them (see page 6) to form irregular bite-size pieces. Bring a medium pot of water to a boil over high heat. Drop the sweet potato into the water and cook them for 3 minutes. Drain the pieces of sweet potato in a colander.

2. In a large bowl, toss the pieces of sweet potato in the cornstarch.

3. In a deep pot, heat at least 3 inches of oil over medium heat. When a wooden chopstick lowered into the oil immediately sizzles (350°F), the oil is ready. Add the pieces of sweet potato and fry them for 5 minutes. Remove them with a spider strainer or slotted spoon.

4. In a wok or large skillet, heat the sugar, water, and 1 tablespoon of oil over medium heat. Continue stirring for 6 to 8 minutes, until the sugar has reduced to a golden syrup. Add the white vinegar, then add sweet potato. Flip everything for a few seconds to coat the sweet potato evenly. Transfer them to a plate immediately.

5. Eat this dish right away before the sugar coating hardens.

PREP TIP: The timing of when to add the sweet potatoes to the sugar syrup is very important. Too early, and you won't get any sugar strands. Too late, and the sweet potatoes will be completely hardened together. Vinegar increases the sugar's elasticity.

PER SERVING: Calories: 345; Total fat: 17g; Saturated fat: 1.5g; Carbohydrates: 47g; Sugar: 28g; Protein: 1g; Calcium: 25mg

琥珀核桃 AMBER WALNUTS

Amber walnuts are a traditional Chinese snack. The name comes from their amber color, and you'll find these sweet, aromatic, and crunchy walnuts absolutely delicious. The same technique can be used with other kinds of nuts, including pecans, cashews, almonds, and peanuts. My favorite thing is to make a variety mix of amber nuts.

PREP TIME:
5 minutes

COOK TIME:
20 minutes

2 cups walnuts

1/2 cup granulated sugar

1/8 teaspoon sea salt

1/3 cup water

1 1/2 cups canola oil

2 tablespoons toasted white sesame seeds

1. Bring a medium pot of water to a boil over high heat. Add the walnuts and blanch them for 3 minutes. Drain the walnuts in a colander.

2. In a wok, combine the sugar, salt, and ⅓ cup of water and heat the mixture over medium heat, stirring with a spatula to dissolve the sugar. Add the walnuts to the wok, flipping them so they're coated in the syrup. Simmer the walnuts for 5 to 7 minutes, uncovered, until all of the water evaporates.

3. With the walnuts still in the wok, add the oil, heat it over medium heat, and fry the walnuts for about 5 minutes, or until their color darkens. As the walnuts fry, flip them constantly to separate them into individual pieces.

4. Using a spider strainer or slotted spoon, transfer the walnuts to a plate. Sprinkle the sesame seeds on top. The walnuts will become crunchy once cooled.

5. Store the walnuts in a sealed glass jar in the pantry for up to 1 week.

PER SERVING: Calories: 512; Total fat: 42g; Saturated fat: 3.5g; Carbohydrates: 32g; Sugar: 26g; Protein: 9g; Calcium: 64mg

Mung Bean Cakes,
PAGE 114

MEASUREMENT CONVERSIONS

VOLUME EQUIVALENTS	U.S. STANDARD	U.S. STANDARD (OUNCES)	METRIC (APPROXIMATE)
LIQUID	2 tablespoons	1 fl. oz.	30 mL
	¼ cup	2 fl. oz.	60 mL
	½ cup	4 fl. oz.	120 mL
	1 cup	8 fl. oz.	240 mL
	1½ cups	12 fl. oz.	355 mL
	2 cups or 1 pint	16 fl. oz.	475 mL
	4 cups or 1 quart	32 fl. oz.	1 L
	1 gallon	128 fl. oz.	4 L
DRY	⅛ teaspoon	—	0.5 mL
	¼ teaspoon	—	1 mL
	½ teaspoon	—	2 mL
	¾ teaspoon	—	4 mL
	1 teaspoon	—	5 mL
	1 tablespoon	—	15 mL
	¼ cup	—	59 mL
	⅓ cup	—	79 mL
	½ cup	—	118 mL
	⅔ cup	—	156 mL
	¾ cup	—	177 mL
	1 cup	—	235 mL
	2 cups or 1 pint	—	475 mL
	3 cups	—	700 mL
	4 cups or 1 quart	—	1 L
	½ gallon	—	2 L
	1 gallon	—	4 L

OVEN TEMPERATURES

FAHRENHEIT	CELSIUS (APPROXIMATE)
250°F	120°C
300°F	150°C
325°F	165°C
350°F	180°C
375°F	190°C
400°F	200°C
425°F	220°C
450°F	230°C

WEIGHT EQUIVALENTS

U.S. STANDARD	METRIC (APPROXIMATE)
½ ounce	15 g
1 ounce	30 g
2 ounces	60 g
4 ounces	115 g
8 ounces	225 g
12 ounces	340 g
16 ounces or 1 pound	455 g

RESOURCES

99 Ranch Market: One of the largest Asian supermarket chains with 54 stores across 10 states, 99 Ranch carries most of the basic ingredients you will need in this book. They have in-store shopping and online shopping (99Ranch.com) and deliver to the 48 contiguous states in the US.

The Mala Market: America's source for premium and hard-to-find Sichuan ingredients and pantry essentials. Products are sold online (TheMalaMarket .com) only. The store ships primarily within the US, but also offers international shipping.

Melissa's Produce: The largest distributor and online retailer (Melissas.com) of specialty produce in the US. They have a selection of harder-to-find Asian vegetables.

Asian Veggies: An online retailer (Asian-Veggies.com) specializing in Asian products. Asian Veggies delivers to NYC and parts of New Jersey and Long Island. They have a great selection of Chinese ingredients, not just vegetables.

Yami: The most popular online retailer (YamiBuy.com) offering one-stop shopping for the Asian American community. They carry a large selection of pantry ingredients and modern kitchen equipment.

Amazon: You can find almost everything you need for the recipes in this book on Amazon (Amazon.com), including fresh vegetables, pantry ingredients, and kitchen tools.

INDEX

Acknowledgments

To my husband, Rajib, and my children, Logan and Connor, thank you for supporting me to follow my dreams over the years! This book would not have happened without you! To my mother, Yanli, you made the biggest impact in my childhood and shaped me into the person I am today. To my loving grandparents, you are my home and the strongest anchor in my life. To oto-san, you were my role model growing up. To uncle Hongbo, the best cook in the family, you are always the funny and affectionate one. Thank you to my great friend, Creag Anderson, for testing many recipes in this book and providing valuable feedback. To my readers and followers, thank you for your encouraging words; they mean the world to me! Lastly, thank you to my editors and the team at Callisto Media for the guidance and opportunity to share these beloved recipes of my heritage.

About the Author

 **Yang Yang** is the voice and photographer behind the popular blog *Yang's Nourishing Kitchen* (YangsNourishingKitchen.com). Originally from Beijing and now living in a suburb of Toronto, Yang shares nutrient-dense, real-food recipes to help her readers achieve balance and well-being. Yang is passionate about traditional food wisdom and cooking practices from the East to the West. She promotes a food philosophy that is about healing our bodies, and she loves to support people wherever they are on their health journey using good food.

Yang also blogs about holistic health, such as her healing stories, traditional Chinese medicine, natural remedies, and the nontoxic lifestyle. Besides writing, she runs fermentation workshops from her home kitchen and works as an independent Beautycounter consultant to help her clients detox by switching to safer skincare and cosmetics. You can find her on Facebook and Instagram at @yangsnourishingkitchen.

CPSIA information can be obtained
at www.ICGtesting.com
Printed in the USA
JSHW011441011221
20881JS00007B/48